Applied Exercise Psychology

*A Practitioner's Guide
to Improving Client Health
and Fitness*

**Mark Anshel, Ph.D.,** is a Professor in the Department of Health, Physical Education and Recreation at Middle Tennessee State University in Murfreesboro, TN. Dr. Anshel has been a professor of sport and exercise psychology and a practicing performance consultant in the fields of sport and exercise for 24 years. In his earlier career he was a director of physical education in the community recreation field. His degrees are from Illinois State University (B.S.) in physical education, and graduate degrees in psychology of human performance from McGill University in Montreal (M.A.), and Florida State University (Ph.D.). He has authored several books including *Sport Psychology: From Theory to Practice* (2003), *Concepts in Fitness: A Balanced Approach to Good Health* (2003), and *Aerobics for Fitness* (1998). His numerous book chapters and research articles have covered topics such as coping with stress, perfectionism, and drug use in sports, and strategies to promote exercise adherence. His current research concerns validating his Disconnected Values Model to improve exercise adherence. Dr. Anshel is a member of the Society of Behavioral Medicine, American Psychological Association, Association for the Advancement of Applied Sport Psychology, and Stress and Anxiety Research Society.

Applied Exercise Psychology

A Practitioner's Guide to Improving Client Health and Fitness

Mark H. Anshel, PhD

SPRINGER PUBLISHING COMPANY

Copyright © 2006 by Springer Publishing Company, Inc.

Springer Publishing Company, Inc.
11 West 42nd Street
New York, NY 10036

Acquisitions Editor: Sheri W. Sussman
Production Editor: Jeanne W. Libby
Cover design by Joanne Honigman
Typeset by International Graphic Services, Inc., Newtown, PA

Library of Congress Cataloging-in-Publication Data

Anshel, Mark H. (Mark Howard), 1948
   Applied exercise psychology : a practitioner's guide to improving client health and fitness / Mark H. Anshel.— 1st ed.
       p. cm.
   Includes bibliographical references and index.
   ISBN 0-8261-3214-6 (soft cover)
   1. Exercise—Psychological aspects. 2. Physical fitness— Psychological aspects. I. Title.
GV481.2.A57 2006
613.7'01'9—dc22

                                                      2005017980

Printed in the United States of America.

This book is dedicated to the memory of my mother, Rochelle, and my father, Bernard, in recognition of their wonderful love and dedication in providing me with the opportunity to learn, to achieve, and with the desire to improve the lives of others. I am honored to be their legacy.

Contents

Preface

$\mathbf{W}$e are in trouble. The health of our country is being compromised due to a lifestyle of overeating and sedentary habits. Never before in our history has the health of so many individuals been put at risk due to the lethal combination of an inactive lifestyle and poor nutrition. It is now apparent that for the first time in U.S. history, our children will lead a shorter, lower quality of life than their parents. The reason? We now live in what health practitioners call an "obesity epidemic." About two-thirds of adults are overweight or obese, costing billions of dollars for related health care treatment.

One group that has been ignored in the fight against overweight and obesity are mental health professionals (MHPs). The MHP is in a very powerful position to promote a healthier lifestyle among their clients. The level of trust and emotional bonding between MHP and client forms a rare opportunity for influencing the thoughts, emotions, and behaviors of persons—clients—who are highly receptive to making positive, constructive, and significant changes in their life. Forming new habits from leading a sedentary lifestyle to becoming more physically active, including regular exercise, requires strong commitment and additional time and energy. Clients perceive their MHP, not unlike their physician, with extraordinary credibility in suggesting lifestyle changes. What have been missing, however, are the knowledge, skills, and willingness of MHPs to play a much larger role in suggesting exercise programs for clients, and the strategies needed to prescribe exercise routines and programs. MHPs often suggest to clients to initiate contact with specialists in beginning an exercise program fully expecting the fitness club industry to meet client needs by providing an informed, high-quality program. Sadly, neither of these expectations—clients contacting fitness clubs and the clubs always offering high-quality programs and leadership—has been met successfully.

Another reason the MHP is in such a strong position to offer prescribed exercise is the strong association between exercise and improved mental health. Numerous studies have clearly shown that mental health conditions related to stress, depression, anxiety, and negative mood state can each be reduced by engaging in a program of regular physical exercise. Evidence of the benefits of physical activity on mental and physical well-being is overwhelming. Yet, many individuals seem to prefer taking prescribed drugs rather than to engage in an activity—exercise—that is both normal and can be very enjoyable. Why do so many individuals make this choice? Why has exercise become so undesirable in our culture?

We have been depending on the wrong professions and industries to help overcome the dilemma of an increasingly unhealthy, overweight society. In all due respect to business owners who provide a needed valuable service to the community, the fitness industry has failed to play a much-needed significant role in improving exercise habits in our communities. Fitness clubs are businesses, first and foremost. Like any business, income is a primary goal, as opposed to looking after the health and welfare of its members over the long term. As a former member of this industry, I can attest to the understandable, yet sad priority given to obtaining memberships, yet providing mere adequate service to members. Instead of giving needed individualized treatment to new club members, most of whom are novice exercisers, typically the new member is given a quick introduction to the equipment and must pay an additional fee for personal training or coaching.

The quality of these trainers is very uneven. Some trainers have solid credentials, a strong knowledge of different types of exercises, proper techniques, and nutrition, and the ability to teach and motivate their clients. These skilled trainers genuinely care about the health and welfare of their clients. They provide valid testing, clear instruction, full observation (as opposed to being distracted by others in the facility), phone their clients for regular updates on their progress or ascertain why the client is absent from a scheduled session, review the client's fitness records, and provide feedback on these observations. In addition, they are concerned about their client's lifestyle, including nutrition, weight control, stress level, and exercise adherence. Other personal trainers, however, are performing this role for additional income, are more interested in their own fitness (or socializing) than in their clients, and do not have the requisite knowledge and communication skills. They rarely speak to their clients outside of the scheduled instructional session for which the client has paid. Although their knowledge of exercise technique may be adequate, their background in related health areas (e.g., nutrition, meeting individual needs and goals) is limited. Buyers beware!

Another group of professionals that has let down the community in promoting health is, ironically, physicians and other medical practitioners. These individuals have the most significant potential to influence patient behavior due to their perceived knowledge and credibility, and yet, they are not encouraging their patients to exercise. The likely reasons include perceived lack of time to counsel patients on the importance of exercise and their fear of offending their patient; physicians loathe disclosing that the likely cause of a patient's illness or poor health data is related to obesity or the lack of exercise. Nurses do not have a specific role or opportunity to provide this information, and, like doctors, are often in similarly poor physical condition as their patients. There is one group of professionals that has been ignored in the war against obesity, yet who possesses a very unique opportunity to change behavior—the MHP.

Another group of professionals that warrants recognition as being part of the problem, rather than the solution, in the fight against obesity and living a sedentary lifestyle is educators. This group includes our physical education teachers, sports coaches, and the school administrators who have eliminated physical education programs from the school curriculum. Thinking back to physical education class and involvement in competitive sports, how many children and adolescents—athletes and nonathletes—were punished by being required to perform push-ups, run laps, and perform other types of exercise? Exercise as a form of punishment has been a tradition in the education system for many years. Yet, associating exercise with teacher/coach disapproval and undesirable student/athlete behaviors has contributed to developing negative attitudes toward physical activity. In addition, hundreds of athletes have personally disclosed to me their unnecessarily rigorous and excessive training regimen. The result is burnout toward engaging in exercise after their sport career is over. The physical education and coaching professions have accomplished exactly the opposite of their mission. Their actions have developed negative, undesirable attitudes toward physical activity rather than their stated mission to promote just the opposite—to view exercise and sports as a healthy, positive, and even necessary lifestyle. In this manner, we have failed our children.

In summary, we have been dependent on various professions (e.g., fitness industry, medical practitioners, health and physical educators, sports coaches) and health-related organizations to provide leadership, information, and opportunities to promote a healthier lifestyle, including more physical activity. Mental health providers have a unique role to influence the behaviors of their clients in the fight against obesity and to increase exercise habits.

For whom was this book written? Any person who in a position of providing counsel or advice to a client or patient will benefit from this book, but primarily for mental health providers (e.g., psychiatrists, psychologists, therapists, counselors, consultants) whose relationship with clients provides a particularly unique opportunity to gain entry for proposing lifestyle changes. Physicians, nurses, physical educators, athletic directors, sports coaches, fitness club owners and managers, personal trainers, organizational consultants, sport psychology consultants, allied health and rehabilitation professionals, and students (graduate and undergraduate) who intend to enter a career in any of the previously mentioned fields will all benefit from this book. It is these individuals who will have an extraordinarily powerful influence on the lives of others with whom they consult in promoting mental and physical health.

Finally, it is important to recognize the importance of a new field of study and practice called exercise psychology. Since 1988 when the *Journal of Sport Psychology* was renamed the *Journal of Sport and Exercise Psychology*, this field of study now has four journals in the English language with the terms "exercise psychology" in the title. The American Psychological Association has a Sport and Exercise Psychology Section, Division 47. One formal definition of exercise psychology is "the study of the brain and behavior in physical activity and exercise settings. Its main focus has been the psychobiological, behavioral, and social cognitive antecedents and consequences of acute and chronic exercise" (Buckworth & Dishman,

2002, p. 17). According to Berger, Pargman, and Weinberg (2002), exercise psychology includes the ways in which exercise alters mood, reduces stress, is a partial treatment in reducing the effects of mental disorders, enhances self-concept and confidence, and can lead to positive or negative addiction/dependence. Readers are invited to see chapter 11 in Anshel (2003b) for an extensive overview of this field.

One related area, however, that has become relatively unexplored is *applied* exercise psychology (Anshel, 2003b, chapter 11). It is this area, aimed for practitioners, that has yet to receive adequate attention by researchers and influence public exercise behavior. Examples of applied exercise psychology include examining effective interventions that influence exercise participation and adherence among healthy and unhealthy populations, designing specific exercise programs that lead to psychological and emotional benefits, studying the psychological predictors of exercise participation and adherence, identifying the effects of cognitive and behavioral strategies on exercise performance, and determining the extent to which exercise influences a person's psychological dispositions—and the mechanisms for these changes. The objective of applied exercise psychology is to determine the efficacy of applying the existing knowledge in this field in explaining, describing, predicting, or changing exercise behavior.

This book contains 13 chapters. Chapter 1 outlines the field of applied exercise psychology. Chapter 2 provides an overview of the reasons we begin and then end exercise regimens, including common exercise barriers. Common theories and models of exercise psychology are presented in chapter 3 to enhance credibility in the field, and to provide a conceptual framework for exercise psychology interventions. Mental health benefits, one popular motive for MHPs to prescribe exercise to clients, are explained in chapter 4. This chapter is especially important for MHPs to recognize the array of psychological benefits of prescribing exercise programs to their clients. Our culture is far too dependent on pharmaceutical agents to combat a host of mental disorders, while ignoring a very natural antidote—exercise. There is vast research support on the benefits of exercise on depression, anxiety, chronic and acute stress, and other undesirable mental conditions. This chapter provides recommendations about how to prescribe exercise programs to address client problems.

Perhaps the most fundamental attitude that leads to exercise engagement is motivation. Chapter 5 provides strategies that promote healthy attitudes about exercise, with a particular focus on developing and maintaining intrinsic motivation. It is important that MHPs who prescribe exercise programs know basic exercise physiology; therefore, chapter 6 provides this information using a narrative that is very readable and understandable. Chapter 7 focuses on prescription strategies to meet different fitness needs, including improving cardiovascular, strength, and flexibility fitness. While fostering a clients' decision to begin an exercise program is the primary goal for MHPs, chapter 8 addresses ways to encourage the secondary goal of maintaining an exercise habit, called exercise adherence. Included in the client population of most MHPs will be individuals with unique characteristics. Special considerations for counseling these clients (e.g., rehabilitation, children, elderly, pregnant women) are covered in chapter 9.

Chapter 10 describes an intervention model that I have developed over the past several years based on my work with corporate clients and, more recently, promoting exercise among university faculty and police officers. It is a very unique approach to exercise participation and adherence because it addresses the link between a person's values (e.g., good health, family) and their negative habits (e.g., not exercising, poor nutrition). When the person determines there is a disconnect between their values and their negative habits, and then acknowledges the costs and long-term consequences of this disconnect, the person must then decide if this disconnect—and its costs and consequences—is acceptable. If it is acceptable, change will not occur. However, if the person concludes this disconnect is unacceptable, they will often feel compelled to replace their negative (unhealthy) habit(s) with new, positive (healthy) routines.

Chapter 11 reviews the array of cognitive and behavioral strategies and program interventions MHPs can use to induce an exercise habit. Chapter 12 reviews ways to create a support system, the qualities of personal trainers, and guidelines for proper programs. Finally, future directions in exercise consulting are discussed in chapter 13. To become more acquainted with the professional literature, a recommended reading list is provided and includes books, journals, and Website resources. The Appendices include an exercise checklist, a list of exercise and health organizations, and ways to measure fitness outcomes. Here's hoping that this book makes a significant impact on your practice and on the lives you touch.

Foreword

I am a licensed clinical psychologist. Chris asked for my last appointment, but arrived late, apologizing, "I couldn't get away from work." This was Chris' first visit. Chris began with safe topics. "I just don't feel well. I have trouble going to sleep. I have a lot of stuff going on at work, and a lot on my mind. I wake up two or three times during the night, and when I get up in the morning I am exhausted. I hate the mornings. I'm tired all the time. My spouse is beginning to irritate me with incessant demands—take the kids to school, get the laundry at the cleaners, remember to get Johnnie's birthday present. I can never do enough."

In a more confessional tone, Chris continued, "To be perfectly honest, my life is coming apart. For the first time ever I don't know what to do. I didn't come here for sympathy or for you to analyze my childhood. I need something practical. I need a plan to feel healthy again. My life is out of control. I put on 15 pounds, and in 9 months my clothes don't fit any more. I feel tense and irritable. I don't rest, and my productivity at work is down, although I am working more than ever before. My love life stinks. I love my family and I love my work, but I'm ready to leave everything. Something has got to change!"

In 35 years of practice as a clinical psychologist, I have seen many men and women reach the end of their rope. Those who practice mental health care are trained to evaluate alcohol abuse, know the signs of depression, deal with marital problems, and many other maladies. We tend to address these problems from a limited professional perspective—psychological, biological, and social, etc. While we value a "holistic" approach to client treatment, and often recommend that our clients "exercise more" to improve their mental and physical health, few practitioners know the *science* or have adequate knowledge to systematically prescribe an exercise program to clients and then monitor and evaluate their progress. These are missing skills in the mental health profession.

Dr. Anshel's book for clients such as Chris and others who would benefit from an intervention of regular exercise in addressing each of this client's clinical problems—stress, alcohol abuse, relationship/marital problems, sexual functioning, need for practical solutions, desire to feel healthy, and being overweight. This is where Dr. Anshel's book, written for mental health professionals, can be very useful in complimenting traditional psychotherapy and other types of cognitive-behavioral interventions.

While we have known for years that exercise improves mental health, there is an absence of education and training for mental health professionals on improving client fitness through exercise. Instead, we recommend our clients "get more exercise," and rely on personal trainers and staff at fitness facilities to provide this service. Sadly, most clients are typically overweight and unfit, feel uncomfortable and physically incapable of performing capably in exercise settings. The barriers of initiating and maintaining an exercise program are extensive. It is often the mental health provider who can be the most influential resource in lifestyle behavior changes.

Every mental health professional, medical practitioner, fitness instructor, and others who promote mental or physical health should read this book. I can attest to the credibility, quality of writing, and clear application of content. Informed mental health practitioners now have information and guidelines for delivering a higher quality of care to their clients.

No one has more credibility and trust in the community to encourage behavior change than mental health professionals. As a clinical psychologist, I am on the front lines in the battle against obesity and our culture's propensity to avoid exercise. *Applied Exercise Psychology* provides guidelines for improving exercise habits and dispelling the myth that lack of exercise, poor nutrition, and the resultant weight gain are the normal evolution of life. Sadly, the premature development of diabetes, heart disease, certain cancers, and reduced quality of life are the result of this thinking.

This book delivers on many fronts. Grounded in science, although not about numbers or a treatise on experimental designs, statistics, critiques of controlled groups, Dr. Anshel instills the empirical findings of *exercise science* into concise principles that can be applied by any well-trained mental health specialist. He serves-up research in a practical, clear, and straightforward manner, and delivers a credible, scientifically based book. This is a clear application of the scientist-practitioner model.

Dr. Anshel articulates principles than can be readily generalized to a wide range of clinical situations. He proposes interventions that are practicable. Anshel is one of the rare researchers who speak the language of the provider. In a subtle and unassuming manner, Dr. Anshel integrates findings of exercise science with the best theories of the behavioral sciences and the principles of behavioral change. Anshel "delivers practice."

Dr. Anshel's unique credentials make him a credible authority on applied exercise psychology. He has co-authored two fitness books, contributed book chapters, and is widely published in scientific journals. His graduate degrees are in sport and exercise psychology. He is a former fitness director in community recreation, and he practiced in Australia as a licensed psychologist. He combines skills and knowledge to provide practitioners with meaningful, scientifically based recommendations to overcome our culture's negative lifestyles.

I am intrigued by his Disconnected Values Model (chapter 10) which provides a behavioral approach to motivating client change in health behavior. The model is based on linking the person's negative habits (e.g., lack of exercise) to his or her values (e.g., health, family), and helping the client identify the disconnect between their habits and values. This model informs one about the costs and long-term consequences of this disconnect, and, if unacceptable, helps the client generate an action plan that replaces the negative habit with positive, health-enhancing routines.

By describing the science that supports applied exercise concepts, and providing guidelines to help initiate, monitor, and adhere to a long-term investment in exercise, Dr. Anshel's book will benefit those mental health, medicine, and fitness professionals on whom we depend to improve our quality of life.

Murphy M. Thomas, Ph.D.
Thomas & Associates, PC
Murfreesboro, TN

Chapter 1

What Is Applied Exercise Psychology?

Individuals who exercise regularly are healthier, feel better, and are less likely to be overweight or obese as compared to individuals who maintain a sedentary lifestyle. Yet, most Western societies remain more sedentary then ever and have abnormally high rates of overweight and obesity. It is apparent that the world, in general, and the U.S., in particular, is getting less and less healthy due to an epidemic of obesity due to overeating and the lack of physical activity. The health of many individuals is at risk because they are unable or unwilling to change their eating and exercise habits.

In the U.S., for instance, about 63% of U.S. men and women are overweight, and about 33% are classified as obese. The likely reasons are an epidemic of the combination of obesity and a sedentary lifestyle, leading to the widespread onset of types 1 and 2 diabetes and hypertension (Nestle & Jacobson, 2000). Approximately 60–70% of adults who begin an exercise program will quit within 6–9 months, despite the widespread belief (82%) that exercise is beneficial to good health. Taken together, the result of these unhealthy habits is a widespread deterioration of quality of life.

In her keynote address at the 2004 Society of Behavioral Medicine Conference in Baltimore, Maryland, Dr. Risa J. Lavizzo-Mourey, President and Chief Executive Officer of the Robert Wood Johnson Foundation, pointed out that for the first time in U.S. history, children today will live a shorter, lower quality of life than their parents. She reported that since 1980, overweight in children, ages 6 to 11, and adolescents, has doubled and tripled, respectively. However, while the causes of obesity are well known, habits that lead to it, specifically poor nutrition and lack of exercise, have proven to be very difficult to change.

Why, then, do so many of us tend to ignore the benefits of physical activity—for ourselves and for our children—and refuse to engage in regular exercise? One problem in overcoming this unhealthy behavior pattern is the development of lifelong, firmly entrenched (negative) habits. Another reason may be the *benefits* associated with *not* exercising. These "benefits" include more time to do other things, not experiencing the unpleasant feelings of fatigue and discomfort, less chance of injury, less expensive if exercising means purchasing special clothing or becoming a fitness club member, and not feeling intimidated or self-conscious when exercising in the presence of others. Of course, however, there are *costs* to leading a sedentary lifestyle. These include poorer general health, lower quality of life, weight gain (including life-threatening obesity), and lower self-esteem—to name a few. When the question is asked, "why do we decide to remain inactive and not engage in regular exercise," the likely reason is because the benefits outweigh the costs (see chapter 10 for additional discussion of the cost-benefit tradeoff).

One group, collectively called *mental health professionals (MHPs)*, which encompasses individuals who provide an array of psychological services, can make a significant impact on improving the health and fitness of many individuals who seek counseling services for various reasons. Given the proven mental and physical benefits of exercise, it would be appear natural to help MHPs become more familiar with the advantages of helping their clients start an exercise program in conjunction with their therapeutic regimen. While everyone needs to exercise regularly, individuals who seek mental health services will particularly benefit from guidance in this area provided by their MHP.

THE NEED FOR THIS BOOK

The genesis of this book is the apparent need to provide MHPs (e.g., psychologists, therapists, counselors, medical personnel, personal trainers) with the guidelines and skills needed to help their clients achieve better physical and mental health and improved quality of life by initiating a long-term commitment to exercise. The willingness of MHPs to embrace a new and exciting role in providing this needed service would result in important ways to improve the health and quality of life of their clients.

DEFINING PHYSICAL ACTIVITY, EXERCISE, AND FITNESS

If mental health professionals are going to help clients develop healthy habits, particularly exercise, they need to be able to communicate important terms and concepts accurately. The three most important concepts in improving client health and well-being are to improve *physical fitness* through *exercise* and other forms of *physical activity*. These terms will be a combination of the most frequently cited definitions from the literature, particularly Corbin and Lindsay (2005).

Physical activity is usually defined as any bodily movement produced by voluntary muscular contractions that results in energy expenditure, usually measured in kilocalories per unit of time. Although it is highly desirable for every person to become more physically active, not all forms of physical activity will improve physical fitness and lead to other desirable health-related outcomes. For example, although taking a slow stroll may have relaxing value and be desirable to reduce stress and recover from a busy day, this form of activity is not considered exercise and will not improve most measures of health that are associated with exercise. The more desirable forms of activity are formally called exercise which leads to physical fitness.

Exercise is a subset, or type, of physical activity that consists of planned, structured, repetitive, bodily movements that a person performs for the purpose of improving or maintaining one or more components of physical fitness or health. Exercise may be *acute*—short term or single bout of activity—or *chronic*—carried out repeatedly over time, preferably several times per week each at various lengths of time.

Physical fitness is a set of attributes that a person possesses to perform physical activity. It is the body's ability to function efficiently and effectively and is comprised of numerous components. *Health-related physical fitness* includes cardiovascular efficiency/endurance, body composition (percent of total body weight that is fat as opposed to lean muscle tissue), muscular strength, and flexibility. *Skill-related fitness* components are ability, balance, coordination, speed, power, and reaction time. *Aerobic fitness* consists of the maximal capacity of the cardiovascular system to take in and use oxygen, also called VO^2 max. Most research that shows improved psychological outcomes, cognitive functioning, and quality of life reflects aerobic forms of physical activity.

DEFINING APPLIED EXERCISE PSYCHOLOGY

A relatively new area of research and application has emerged in recent years called *exercise psychology*, or more recently, *applied exercise psychology*. Exercise psychology is defined as "the study of psychological factors underlying participation and adherence in physical activity programs" (Anshel et al., 1991, p. 56). Lox, Martin, and Petruzzelle (2003) define exercise psychology as "concerned with (a) the application of psychological principles to the promotion and maintenance of leisure physical activity (exercise), and (b) the psychological and emotional consequences of leisure physical activity" (p. 5). Exercise psychology differs from sport psychology primarily concerning the nature of the population—athletes versus exercise participants, the type of physical activity—sport versus exercise, and the goals of that activity—improved health and fitness versus optimal athletic performance and successful outcomes. Both areas consist of attempts that explain, describe, and predict behavior.

According to Berger, Pargman, and Weinberg (2002), exercise psychology includes the ways in which exercise alters mood, reduces stress, is a partial treatment to reducing the effects of mental disorders, enhances self-concept and confidence, and can lead to positive or negative addiction/dependence. Other effects from increased aerobic training include reduced acute and chronic anxiety, reduced chronic depression, improved both acute and chronic pain tolerance, reduced ratings of perceived exertion (explained later), and improved quality of life. In an expansion of this description, Buckworth and Dishman (2002) also include "psychobiological, behavioral, and social cognitive antecedents and consequences of acute and chronic exercise" (p. 17). By *antecedents*, the authors include which factors will predict who will engage in an ongoing habit of exercise and who will quit. The term *consequences* reflects the study of exercise outcomes, that is, the ways in which exercise (both short term, also called acute, and long term, also referred to as chronic) influences mental and emotional processes. The effect of mental skills on exercise performance is also included in this definition. For example, as discussed later, thinking positive thoughts (e.g., "I feel good" or "stay with it") will result in better endurance than thinking negative thoughts (e.g., "I don't like this" or "when will this be over?"). While there is a growing body of research in exercise psychology, a neglected aspect of this field has been to examine the effectiveness of research findings, theories, and models in exercise settings. It is this area—applying the exercise and sport psychology literature in exercise settings, and going beyond the theories and research findings—that is the focus of this chapter.

Researchers, educators, and practitioners need insights into the psychological benefits of exercise, the reasons some of us exercise while others choose to be inactive, the reasons why others begin an exercise program and then quit, and what each of us can do to start and maintain a regular exercise regimen, a concept called adherence, and to offer suggestions about how mental skills can be used to improve exercise performance. An extensive review of the literature (e.g., Berger, Pargman, & Weinberg, 2002; Buckworth & Dishman, 2002) reveals the following list of areas that define the field of exercise psychology.

- Designing specific exercise programs for experiencing psychological benefits;

- Examining positive addiction and commitment to exercise;

- Understanding the causes and antecedents of negative addiction to exercise, in which excessive physical activity leads to injury, eating disorders resulting in excessive weight loss, social isolation, exercising when sick, or feeling depressed or anxious (worried) if an exercise session is missed;

- Studying the psychological predictors (dispositions and personality profile) of who will and will not engage in regular exercise;

- Determining the effects of short-term (acute) and long-term (chronic) exercise on changes in mood state;

- Measuring changes in selected personal dispositions due to exercise, such as various dimensions of self-esteem, confidence, optimism, and anxiety;

- Identifying the psychological benefits of regular exercise;

- Exercising to improve quality of life;

- Prescribing exercise as a tool in psychotherapy (e.g., depression, anxiety, emotional disturbances) for specific populations, such as children, elderly, physically disabled;

- Using exercise in rehabilitation settings (e.g., recovery from injury, cardiac or pulmonary disease);

- Predisposing factors that explain the exercise high, flow, and peak experience and how to facilitate these feelings;

- Studying the effectiveness of mental skills that improve exercise performance;

- Examining the effectiveness of cognitive and behavioral techniques that promote exercise participation and adherence;

- Predict exercise adherence and dropout; and

- Prescribing exercise as a stress management strategy.

The principles, concepts, and theories that describe, explain, and predict sport performance also apply to all forms of human performance, including exercise. There is now more research, articles, books, and job opportunities related to factors that contribute to exercise participation and nonparticipation, partly due to an increasingly overweight, inactive, unhealthy population. The need to understand the reasons for these very unfortunate trends, particularly related to explaining a person's sedentary lifestyle, and studying effective interventions that promote exercise behavior, is growing.

In summary, exercise psychology is comprised of several components. I've identified six areas of study and application: (1) exercise motivation, (2) exercise adherence and compliance, (3) use of cognitive and behavioral strategies that promote exercise participation, (4) strategies that foster exercise performance, (5) ways in which exercise influences mood and psychological well-being, and (6) effective exercise leadership. These areas will be discussed in depth throughout the book.

EXERCISE PSYCHOLOGY CONSULTING: A VOID IN THE FIELD

It is an established fact that exercise improves mental health. We feel better when engaging in a regular program of physical activity, particularly aerobic-type exercise in which the heart rate is elevated significantly. Aerobic exercise consists of engaging in physical activity over a relatively prolonged time period, during which time heart rate remains consistently elevated. Aerobic exercise, and to a lesser extent, resistance training and brisk walking, have been shown to improve mood state, enhance self-esteem and confidence, reduce depression, chronic and acute anxiety, and psycho-social stress, and promote recovery from unpleasant events in one's life.

The results of intervention studies on promoting exercise behavior as a permanent behavior change, called *exercise adherence*, have been equivocal (Buckworth & Dishman, 2002). Most individuals who start an exercise program discontinue their participation within three to six months. Adherence to healthy behaviors has challenged researchers and practitioners for many years. Sackett (1976), for example, found that scheduled appointments for medical treatment are missed 20 to 50% of the time, and that about 50% of patients are remiss in taking their medications as prescribed by their physician. After 6 months, other health-related behaviors (e.g., smoking cessation, dietary restrictions, weight control strategies) have an adherence rate of below 50%.

The focus of psychological consulting is to improve a person's state of mind and improve quality of life. Both cognitive and behavioral approaches are usually taken in the consulting process to meet a client's needs. While counseling and clinical training provide a broad overview of the techniques to promote mental health, the graduate student is not trained in providing guidance in helping clients start and maintain a fundamental behavioral strategy—exercise. The purpose for this book is an attempt to overcome this deficiency in the education and training of psychologists and others who provide counsel to a sedentary and relatively unhealthy society. Who, then, is consulting exercise participants, and why do psychologists need to become involved?

The Issue of Title: Who Is an Exercise Psychologist?

If practitioners in sport psychology are called sport psychologists, sport psychology consultants/counselors, or mental skills coaches, do similar titles apply to individuals who work in exercise settings? Are there exercise psychologists/counselors/coaches? Berger et al. (2002) use the terms *exercise psychologist* on numerous occasions. Yet, this title may not be correct. Lets start with the title *psychologist*. As the authors duly note, the title psychologist is legally protected, and requires that the professional be licensed by their State Board of Licensed Psychologists (each state may have a similar, but not identical, board identification) to practice psychology in the state in which they reside and practice. In addition, graduate psychology programs that result in licensure do not include courses in the exercise sciences. Consequently, graduate students would not have completed a course in exercise psychology. Thus, licensed psychologists are rarely trained to work in exercise settings, or to have mastered the professional literature in providing counsel to promote participation in and adherence to exercise programs. Perhaps in a clinical population, in which exercise is a vehicle that provides a desirable treatment to overcome mental illness or some other psychopathology, students may have received information on the benefits of exercise. Until university programs are in place to provide course work and clinical training for working with clients in exercise settings or who wish to engage in exercise, the term "exercise psychologist" is not very practical. Perhaps a more accurate and valuable title is "exercise (or mental skills) counselor, consultant, or coach," referring to a person trained in the exercise sciences, who is familiar with the sport and exercise literature, and can provide guidance and nonclinical interventions to clients.

DEFINING KEY TERMS

Consulting clients to engage in regular exercise requires mastery of fundamental concepts and terms. This is important for explaining to clients the different types of exercises, their purposes and expected outcomes, and how to meet the client's personal needs (see Anshel, Reeves, & Roth, 2003).

Exercise

A form of leisure physical activity (as opposed to occupational or household physical activity) that is undertaken to achieve a particular objective such as reduced stress, improved fitness and health, improved physical appearance, and so on.

Physical Activity

All bodily movement that cause increases in physical exertion beyond that which occurs during normal activities of daily living.

Cardiovascular (Aerobic) Fitness

Efficiency of the heart, lungs, and blood vessels to supply nutrients to the body. This type of fitness is reached through aerobic types of exercise (e.g., jogging, swimming, brisk walking) over a prolonged time period, usually 20 to 45 minutes. It is the best way to burn calories and reduce or maintain body weight.

Flexibility

The functional range of motion of a certain joint and its corresponding muscle groups. Greater flexibility reduces the chance of joint-related injuries and stiffness.

Muscular Strength

The ability of a muscle to exert force against a resistance. Stronger muscles prevent or reduce the severity of an injury. Muscular strength, gained through resistance training, increases the percent of weight that is *lean muscle*, which is desirable. More muscle increases metabolism, that is, the number of calories burned at rest to sustain life. Improved bone mass (i.e., stronger bones) also results from resistance training.

Body Composition

Consists of two components, the percentage of your body weight that is body fat and the percentage of your body weight that is lean body tissue (muscle, organs, bones, and bodily fluids).

In summary, it is essential that MHPs become familiar with essential concepts that will allow them to provide valuable and insightful counsel to their clients—individuals who will benefit immeasurably from embarking on an exercise program. Why is the MHP so important in helping clients to start exercising? Let's view the exercise experience through the eyes of any novice exerciser. Starting an activity that will induce physical stress and discomfort, often in an environment filled with individuals who are younger and in better physical condition, is very intimidating. Clients will often be filled with uncertainty, anxiety, self-consciousness, and possess a lack of knowledge and skill about proper exercise technique. In addition, they will be experiencing physical discomfort that will be exacerbated by using improper methods (e.g., lack of proper warm-up, negative self-talk, lack of proper pacing). It is no wonder that at least half of all individuals who begin an exercise program drop out within six months.

The MHP has spent considerable time and energy in establishing trust and mutual respect with his or her clients. The goal is to help clients feel the self-motivation needed to take the necessary risks of embarking on a new and uncertain adventure—changing from a sedentary to a more active and healthier lifestyle. At the same time, the client's mental disposition will go from unpleasant to pleasant emotions and dispositions, a particularly important issue for many clients who seek counsel. The MHP is in a unique position to provide both emotional support and information to clients in providing guidance and leadership toward starting an exercise program. Certainly the health and fitness industry are not performing this function at optimal efficiency. The information provided in this book will assist the MHP to have an important role in fostering new exercise rituals among their clients and improve both mental and physical health in the process.

Chapter 2

Exercise Barriers: Why We Do Not Enjoy Physical Activity

Helping individuals begin a habit of regular exercise is like herding a group of feral cats; it's virtually impossible. Or so it seems. I have worked for over 25 years with individuals who want to begin an exercise program, and I have heard every excuse why a person chooses not to exercise regularly. The most common excuse is lack of time. In response to this excuse, the client should consider this: There are 168 hours in a week. A proper fitness program that includes cardiovascular exercise should consume about 3 hours per week. Three hours is just 1% of 168. That's all it takes—just 1% of a person's time. Therefore, lack of time is not the *real* reason individuals do not exercise. Instead, it is the *perception* of lack of time that is the culprit.

EXERCISE BARRIERS

Nevertheless, MHPs need to understand the sources of reasons clients have failed to prioritize their schedule to accommodate regular exercise. These "reasons" are called exercise barriers. In this chapter, I will examine the reasons people do exercise, and the reasons they do not—the common barriers to starting an exercise program. The reasons for dropping out of exercise after they begin will be covered in chapter 8 on exercise adherence. Before addressing the motives for and against exercising, I want to offer possible explanations for a negative attitude toward physical activity.

Why We Do Not Enjoy Exercise

The Burned Out Former Athlete

Sports coaches can be cruel. While physical training and getting "in shape" is an important feature of successful sports performance, sometimes a coach will exercise an athlete "to death." Not literally, of course, although athlete deaths from excessive exercise occur every year, especially in hot weather. In this instance, however, I refer to overtraining. Coaches simply require the athletes to perform too much exercise to the point where the athlete develops a very negative attitude toward it. The consequence of "exercise burnout" among sports competitors is that when they have completed their athletic careers, they are unlikely to stay in shape, or even perform regular moderate exercise again. I have discussed this problem with many athletes and they all tend to agree that they have not engaged in regular exercise following the end of their career. Excessive weight gain is one result of this negative attitude.

Exercise as Punishment

Our physical education teachers and sports coaches can take a collective bow on this issue as the culprits that contribute to negative attitudes toward exercise. Time and time again, physical education teachers and coaches have used exercise as punishment starting in grade school to discipline inappropriate student/athlete behavior. If the student was late to class or made a performance error, the student was "commanded" to run, do push-ups, or perform some other physically demanding task. By associating exercise with undesirable behavior, this form of punishment fosters a negative attitude toward exercise; instead of fun, exercise is a reminder of what *not* to do.

Injury

Fair enough. It is wrong to exercise when injured. Tissue damage can become more extensive. You have to "listen to your body," rest and heal if injured. Nevertheless, sometimes pain is more fiction (phantom) than fact. We are more susceptible to pain because of our overweight and under-exercised status. Past studies have shown that fitness, both aerobic and strength-related, improves stability around joints and makes us less likely to feel physical discomfort. In addition, unfit individuals have a lower pain threshold than their more fit counterparts (Anshel & Russell, 1994).

Lack of Fitness Knowledge

Exercising correctly consists of techniques that must be learned and practiced. Proper instruction on getting started in your fitness program, correct methods to lift weights, and proper ways to become aerobically fit without unnecessary stress and injury help prevent dropout. This rarely happens, however. Novices pay their membership fee at a fitness club, and then are left to use the facilities on their own, not knowing proper protocol nor given any incentive to keep going. The fitness club industry, a business enterprise, is shameless when it comes to looking after the health and welfare of their members. No wonder the membership retention rate is so low.

Unpleasant Sensations From Vigorous Physical Activity

For many individuals, the feeling of being physically active is unpleasant, if not unbearable. There are several reasons for this. First, we are who we train to be. If an individual leads a sedentary lifestyle and becomes overweight, his or her body is accustomed to be comfortable with that lifestyle. The body's physiology will be uncomfortable with heightened physical exertion. It does not help that most individuals do not receive guidance and instruction on proper exercise techniques, thereby exacerbating the problems associated with exertion. Finally, the body types of some individuals are simply not compatible with aerobic-type exercise. A person's body is categorized as ectomorph (slight build), mesomorph (medium build), and endomorph (heavy build). This is collectively called *somatotype*. Persons with an endomorph body type (e.g., football linemen, wrestlers) have great difficulty with aerobic activity—sustained physical exertion. They are built for quick, rapid acceleration tasks. Thus, body type partially explains a persons' attraction toward a certain type of exercise.

Our Sedentary Lifestyle

There is not a better exercise barrier in explaining the propensity to avoid exercise than the fact that our culture breeds inactivity. Europeans, Scandinavians, Africans, and Asians, among others, are often amazed at a lifestyle that encourages consumption of large amounts of food, while remaining as physically inactive as possible. Look at us while we stand on an escalator going *down*. Moving is almost sacrilegious. The consequence is an epidemic of overweight and obese individuals that will result in poorer health and shorter lifespan. This is why it is so important to encourage clients to move—to do anything active such as gardening, walking stairs, riding a bicycle—anything that encourages physical activity. When it comes to structured exercise, it is imperative to start slow, than build up our resistance to fatigue and discomfort. Leading an active lifestyle will help overcome our refusal to move more than we must and why we find exercise so undesirable.

Common Barriers to Exercise Participation

There are reasons, good and bad, valid and invalid, that explain a person's decision to engage or not engage in regular exercise. Here are the most common and, sometimes, valid barriers.

Convenience/Availability

Clearly, a person who perceives a workout facility as convenient is more likely to exercise at that facility than if there is a perception of the facility being inconvenient. It is the individual's *perception* of a conveniently located facility rather than the actual proximity of the facility that is most important in determining exercise behavior (Sallis & Hovell, 1990).

Environmental Factors

The geographical location, climate, and neighborhood of a facility will influence exercise behavior. Extreme temperatures, precipitation, or an unsafe environment all form valid reasons to avoid exercising.

Physical Limitations

Experiencing injury, extreme discomfort, overweight or obesity, disease, and physical fatigue are reasons to avoid exercise. The novice exerciser must be patient in trying to reach fitness-related goals, and to slowly build endurance and resistance to fatigue.

Lack of Time

Addressed earlier in this chapter, the perceived lack of time is a primary excuse to avoid exercise. The facts are that individuals citing lack of time as a primary reason for not exercising are really exhibiting poor time management skills. Think about what a person would need to sacrifice in "free time" activities in order to take 3 hours a week to exercise: less television, fewer or shorter phone calls and e-mail messages, slight reduction of time for social gathering, or fewer meals out, all of which consume an extensive amount of time and energy. There are several strategies a person can do to overcome the "not enough time" barrier (discussed later).

Boredom or Lack of Enjoyment

For many individuals, physical activity is both unpleasant and unexciting. Imagine an overweight individual leading a sedentary lifestyle walking alone around a track for 20–30 minutes? How about a person riding a stationary bicycle while perspiring and trying to catch his or her breath? Neither of these images creates a sense of excitement and enjoyment to the exerciser whose exercise history may be limited and whose current fitness level and body weight makes this undertaking stressful and undesirable. Because so few exercise beginners recruit a performance coach or are given proper instruction, it is no wonder the dropout rate for exercise novices is so high.

Excessive or Unachievable Goals

Far too many exercise novices want to look like a favorite model or film star, or want to meet the expectations of others or meet a goal that is unrealistic, perhaps even dangerous. In fact, a goal such as losing a large amount of weight in a relatively short time due to a new exercise program may be potentially fatal. Sadly, it is not uncommon for a person to "make up" for missing weeks or even years of exercise by engaging in a highly intense program that leads to cardiac arrest, even death.

It took years to become an overweight, unfit individual and changing this status will not take just a few weeks. It is fair to say, however, that research in the exercise physiology literature concerning the time needed to markedly improve fitness after beginning an exercise program is from 4 to 6 weeks (ACSM, 2001). This also marks the time frame when exercise exertion will feel less intense; there will not be the same feeling of struggle and discomfort. Therefore, MHPs want to encourage their clients to exercise at least three times a week for four weeks so that they can begin to notice more pleasant, fewer undesirable side effects from physical exertion.

Lack of Confidence

In my study (Anshel, 2003a) on the effect of self-monitoring strategies on exercise adherence among the faculty and staff employed at my university, I personally interviewed all 103 participants. Among the questions asked was "What factors would lead you to quit exercising and withdraw from this 8-week study?" They were asked to indicate the perceived barriers of adhering to the exercise program. Almost 60% of the respondents indicated lack of confidence, and the need for personal coaching and instruction.

Lack of Instruction and Coaching

How can we expect individuals to feel safe, secure, and motivated to pursue an exercise program unless they possess the requisite knowledge and skill? Yet, this is exactly what we do. We have wonderful exercise programs and facilities in most towns and cities, yet we spend relatively little time introducing new exercisers to the equipment, proper methods of exercise, and skills needed to avoid injury and obtain the maximal benefits of their program. No wonder the exercise dropout rate is so high. The research literature (e.g., general psychology, sport psychology) clearly indicates that it is human nature to withdraw from activities in which we do not achieve success or perceive ourselves as competent, a concept called achievement motivation (Anshel, 2003b). Unless we provide a comfortable, non-threatening environment in which to offer instruction to novice exercisers we can expect high dropout rates from exercise programs.

Perceived Lack of Improvement

Returning to the theme of perceived competence (which leads to intrinsic motivation), persisting in an activity such as exercise is often based on the perception of improved skills, superior performance outcomes, or that the level of physical exertion is lower (i.e., exercising is getting easier). This is why exercise pre-testing, to establish a fitness baseline prior to starting a program, has long-term motivational value. Comparing baseline scores with subsequent test scores demonstrates improvement (achievement).

Absence of Social Support

There is an extensive research base that clearly shows the high motivational value of social support in exercise participation and adherence (Anshel, Reeves, & Roth, 2003). Social support includes positive reinforcement—verbal and nonverbal—from partners, family, and friends, exercising with a friend, obtaining instruction or coaching, or exercising in an environment that is generally positive and comfortable. Learning a new set of (exercise) skills, visiting a location that is unfamiliar or threatening (e.g., fitness facility), or engaging in a task that requires considerable effort are all predictors of disengagement—starting and then quitting the activity. Social support, then, is the antidote of these factors; a virtual mandate for exercise novices.

Taken together, there is no shortage of barriers that will prevent individuals from starting or maintaining their exercise program. Sadly, our unfit and overweight population is making it increasingly difficult to enjoy the challenge of becoming fitter, leaner, and healthier. The good news, however, is that MHPs are in a position to help the transition of their clients from unfit and inactive, among other undesirable characteristics, into persons who are both physically and mentally healthier. The MHP can become the client's own "performance coach" by providing the initial information and strategies to overcome perceived barriers to exercise.

EXERCISE MOTIVATION

Why We Exercise

Before we can begin dealing with the barriers for exercising, we need to examine the various reasons many individuals choose to exercise regularly. How are they different from their sedentary counterparts? What causes an exerciser to engage in that ritual, while others choose to ignore it? Why do some individuals embrace the words (and actions) of Dr. Robert Hutchinson, the former President at the University of Chicago, who said, "Every time I feel like exercising I lie down until the feeling passes"? Despite such sentiments that are no doubt shared by many individuals, there are situational and personal factors that promote exercise behavior—and statistically predict it. They are as follows (unranked in importance):

Physique Self-Esteem

Self-esteem, the extent to which a person values him or herself, is critical to explaining and predicting behavior. As MHPs know, there are several dimensions and sources of self-esteem, one of which is the body. Individuals who value their health, their physique, and whose goal it is to improve and maintain their physical appearance have high physique self-esteem. These individuals are more likely to exercise than their low physique self-esteem counterparts. Improved fitness increases physique self-esteem.

Weight Control

It's common knowledge that many countries in the Western world suffer from an obesity epidemic. As indicated earlier, as a culture, we are eating too much food (especially late at night) and remaining sedentary. Regular exercise is simply not part of our daily routine. Still, one important motive for engaging in exercise is to help control weight—and it does. However, weight may not come off easily, because muscle weighs more than fat, and we add muscle through exercise. The literature (e.g., Blair & Brodney, 1999) clearly indicates that we gain the same medical benefits from exercise whether or not we are overweight or obese. As the authors of their meta-analysis found, "active obese individuals actually have lower morbidity and mortality than normal weight individuals who are sedentary" (p.

S646). MHPs should remind their clients that exercise has many health benefits whether or not they are losing weight.

Affiliation/Social Benefits

Anytime people gather at a given location or share similar interests, they tend to interact based on shared interests. Exercise is no exception. Fitness classes, weight training, yoga, running clubs, or simply attending a fitness center or health club are examples of programs in which the primary motive for attending includes a strong social component. As Markland and Ingledew (1997) found in their development of the Exercise Motivation Inventory, social affiliation is a strong predictor of exercise motivation and persistence. This is one reason the MHP wants to ensure that, if a client plans to attend an exercise facility, that he or she receive social support by exercising with a friend, will be introduced to other patrons, or will receive personal coaching at the venue.

Improved Health

Naturally, one motive for exercising is to improve or maintain physical and mental health. The health belief model (HBM) posits that individuals who associate exercise with improved health and well being are more likely to begin and maintain an exercise program than persons who do not make this association. Sadly, the HBM has received uneven support in previous studies. Many sedentary individuals, some of whom at one time started and then quit an exercise program, still believe in its health benefits. Thus, it is wrong to assume that clients will be more inclined to exercise just because they believe that exercise improves health and well-being.

One way to enhance the motivation for exercise based on improved health is to provide clients with health-related data. The strongest motivator to change behavior for many individuals is to acknowledge that their health is at risk due to a current characteristic (e.g., overweight, obesity) or medical problem (e.g., poor results on cholesterol testing), and that the best way to improve their health status is to increase the amount of daily physical activity.

Ill Health Avoidance

For many individuals, the desire to improve health is *less* motivating than wanting to avoid poor health and disease. Because clients tend to strongly value their family and career, developing an illness or disease would be devastating. Few individuals would continue to act in a way that would lead to ill health or premature death, considering the importance of their family, among other values. Guilt, pain, and fear of being a burden to family and other healthcare givers are related motivators to avoid ill health. Exercise becomes more desirable.

Improved Fitness

For many individuals, improving fitness level becomes a very desirable goal. We look, feel, and perform better when our fitness improves. These desirable outcomes of a regular exercise create a sense of competence and satisfaction that form the basis of intrinsic motivation (Anshel, 2003b). Improved fitness becomes its own reward. This is why fitness test scores (e.g., numerical data on aerobic or strength performance) have great motivational value and should be included at the start of an exercise program.

Stress Management

There are several explanations for linking exercise to reduced stress, as shown in numerous studies. Perhaps the most apparent explanation, the distraction hypothesis, is that exercise distracts us from thoughts and tasks that are perceived as stressful. Exercise also changes our biochemistry (e.g., endorphins), improves mood state, and provides a general feeling of well-being. Sadly, stressed clients will contend they have no time for exercise, when, in fact, exercise will likely "de-stress" them.

Competitiveness

For individuals who have a competitive orientation, exercise can be a form of intra-individual competition. Running speed or endurance, amount or repetitions of lifting weights, weight loss, percent body fat reduced, and fitness test scores are all examples of opportunities to compare previous with current performance, a form of competition that may increase a person's drive to exceed their current fitness level.

In summary, there are many sources of motivation that MHPs can recognize in helping to promote a client's motivation to start and adhere to an exercise program. In addition to knowing their client's personal needs and characteristics, MHPs should offer a checklist of motives for exercising. The MHP would help clients designate which of these motives is most important, perhaps in rank order, then formulate a plan to carry out the exercise program, keeping in mind the primary source of exercise motivation.

Chapter 3

Theories and Models
of Exercise Behavior

No doubt some practitioners question the usefulness of theories and models for contributing to their skills as MHPs. It's true that selected theories are meant to advance knowledge of a field of study, yet have minimal value in applied settings. However, we need theories and models to: (a) explain behavioral phenomena, (b) predict future behavior, (c) reduce an abundance of information into a framework that is organized and understandable, (d) to provide guidelines for testing the effectiveness of interventions, and (e) generalize results of studies to specific populations. MHPs who aspire to expand their career into the field of applied exercise psychology need to understand the foundations of health and exercise behavior, to be able to interpret client behaviors, and to apply selected aspects of the theory in practice. This chapter serves two purposes: (1) to briefly explain the best-known theories and models in describing, explaining, and predicting health and exercise behavior, and (2) to apply these theories and models in exercise settings for the practitioner.

BRIEF REVIEW AND CRITIQUE OF HEALTH AND
EXERCISE BEHAVIOR THEORIES AND MODELS

Most researchers and practitioners (e.g., Clark & Becker, 1998; Ockene, 2001) agree that the reasons individuals voluntarily engage in health behavior change are due to: (1) preventing illness or promoting health behavior, (2) disease management, that is to obtain a diagnosis and to discover suitable treatment, and (3) to receive treatment in restoring health or at reducing disease progression. An array of models and theories have been published over the years that reflect these motives for enhancing health and well-being, each mediated by environmental and social conditions. Each theory or model has been met with limited success in promoting behavior change, particularly with respect to initiating and maintaining exercise behavior. One limitation of this research has been the reliance on theories and models in which it is assumed that the person *desires* a change in behavior. The following section will examine the likely reasons for these equivocal findings and to suggest a "missing link" in previous attempts to encourage exercise behavior.

Health Belief Model (HBM)

The HBM (Becker & Maiman, 1975) is based on the premise that persons are more likely to engage in behaviors they perceive as healthy. Conversely, actions will be avoided if they ostensibly will lead to unhealthy outcomes. Thus, the perception that engaging in regular exercise will prevent or control poor health, excessive weight gain, and other undesirable outcomes will encourage exercise behavior. HBM increasingly predicts that a person will initiate healthy behaviors, including exercise, if he or she is concerned about their health, feel susceptible to, or are currently experiencing, health problems, feel empowered to prevent or control health problems, or believe that exercise will reduce the likelihood of becoming ill or unhealthy.

The HBM has received moderate support by researchers. In their review of literature, Berger, Pargman, and Weinberg (2002) concluded that the HBM was most predictive of health-related behaviors among younger populations. In a test of the HBM to predict dropouts and compliers among cardiac rehabilitation patients, Oldridge and Streiner (1990) found that the HBM correctly classified 80% of the patients. The most important predictors of continuing versus stopping regular exercise was perceived exercise effectiveness and improved general health. Clearly, the HBM can predict exercise participation only to the extent that an individual links exercise habits with improved health. This is quite a challenge, however, to individuals who do not perceive their health as at risk. Adolescents and young adults, for example, are known to engage more frequently in high-risk behaviors, such as tobacco, drug, and alcohol use, and faster driving habits. Additional, more current research is needed to test the model among older age groups, both healthy and unhealthy populations.

Another limitation of the HBM is that this model is based on avoiding illness rather than explaining exercise behavior (Buckworth & Dishman, 2002). Buckworth and Dishman contend that "the HBM is more useful for preventive health behaviors and compliance with medical regiments, and less successful when applied to exercise" (p. 224). Studies have shown, in fact, that perceived susceptibility was inversely associated with exercise adherence. This suggests that physical activity and exercise are not universally perceived as health behaviors, or that perceiving exercise as healthy does not necessarily translate into actually *doing* exercise. In addition to health-related reasons, people also exercise for purposes of social interaction, enjoyment, stress reduction, competition, and improved physical appearance. Finally, not unlike most theories and models, the HBM avoids suggesting intervention strategies to promote exercise participation and adherence. Thus, HBM does not adequately explain low exercise adherence.

Theories of Reasoned Action and Planned Behavior

The theory of planned behavior (TPB) is an extension and modification of the theory of reasoned action (TRA; Ajzen & Fishbein, 1974). The primary question addressed by the TRA and TPB concerns the factors that influence an individual's decisions about their behavior in social settings. TRA posits that behavioral decisions are based on information and beliefs about the appropriateness of their actions, the outcome they expect from their actions, and the importance they place on these outcomes. The most important component of TRA, however, is that the person's *intentions* form the best predictors of actual behavior. The intention to perform certain actions reflects the person's *attitudes* about the behavior and about *subjective, social norms* of that behavior. The attitude toward exercise, for instance, reflects the individual's beliefs about the benefits and consequences—positive and negative evaluations—of engaging or not engaging in regular exercise.

The second component of TRA consists of subjective, social norms about the behavior. This reflects the individual's perceptions about the importance that *others* place on the behavior and the person's incentive to meet others' expectations. Thus, a person who is surrounded by one or more friends or family members who habitually exercise is more likely to exercise regularly than an individual whose friends and family do not (Anshel, 2003b). It is understandable, then, that developing social links as part of an exercise program (e.g., hiring a physical trainer, working out with friends, socializing at fitness clubs, training with teammates) often results in better exercise adherence. As Ajzen and Fishbein (1974) conclude, sometimes attitude is the primary predictor of intentions, while other times it is the social norm component.

In his modified follow-up of TRA, Ajzen (1985) added a third component to predicting exercise behavior—perceived behavioral control, that is, an individual's perception that he or she has the resources (i.e., skill and ability) and the opportunity to perform the behavior or to attain the goal. Thus, an individual with unrealistic expectations about their exercise performance or outcome will likely result in low perceived control. These unmet expectations, in turn, will lead to disappointment and feelings of helplessness (i.e., low self-control) about their apparent inability to meet their fitness-related goals. Quitting future exercise participation may result. In summary, then, TRA and TPB posit that a person who does not believe that exercise participation will produce the needed benefits or perceive that others do not wish that they participate are less likely to be physically active. The belief that exercise will not result in meeting desired goals or have intended benefits, or that past exercise experiences were unpleasant (e.g., athletes who feel burned out from overtraining; students who are forced to exercise by their physical education teacher as a form of punishment) will result in negative attitudes toward physical activity.

In a meta-analysis to determine the extent to which TRA and TPB successfully predicted exercise behavior, Hausenblas, Carron, and Mack (1997) found that attitude strongly influences intention to exercise, and that intention to exercise predicts exercise behavior. However, one moderator variable of this link is the individual's perceived control over their behavior. Thus, according to Hausenblas et al. (1997), "individuals have the greatest commitment to exercise when they hold favorable beliefs about exercise and believe that they can successfully perform the behavior" (p. 45). Ironically, these favorable beliefs, or attitudes, toward exercise, also form one limitation of the model.

As Buckworth and Dishman (2002) contend, a person may believe exercise is very healthy and desirable, yet conclude that there is a lack of time in the day to exercise regularly. In addition, the results of several studies have shown that intention to exercise does not account for all exercise behavior (Mackinnon, Ritchie, Hooper, & Abernethy, 2003). Finally, other common barriers to exercise have been well established in the previous literature (e.g., physical discomfort, lack of a convenient exercise facility, intimidation of observers), each of which is accompanied by the person's very positive attitudes toward engaging in regular exercise (Lox, Martin, & Petruzzello, 2003).

The components of TRA and TPB, the person's intention to exercise and their perceived behavioral control, do not necessarily predict exercise behavior. Persons must first develop a favorable attitude toward exercise, no easy task in a sedentary culture. However, understanding the benefits of exercising and the costs of not exercising will help promote a desirable attitude to initiate and maintain an exercise program. Finally, while TRA and TPB may provide the factors that enhance the likelihood of engaging in regular exercise, there are no implications for behavioral interventions in promoting the person's initiation and adherence to exercise.

Self-Efficacy Theory

Self-efficacy is a set of beliefs and expectations about how capable a person feels in performing the necessary behaviors to achieve a desirable outcome (Bandura, 1997). Self-efficacy is specific to a behavior and situation. A person can feel high self-efficacy about their ability to gain strength through weight training, yet feel low self-efficacy when it comes to performing aerobic exercise. High self-efficacy about the activity results in a higher likelihood the person will engage in that activity, but this feeling will not necessarily be generalized to other types of tasks (e.g., competitive sport versus exercise) or situations (e.g., running competition). Not surprisingly, individuals who believe that they are capable of performing the required actions to meet situational demands will more likely engage in those actions. These expectations affect people's selection of those activities, the degree of effort expended on the activities, and the extent to which they will persist at the activities, especially after experiencing failure and the unpleasant consequences of not meeting expectations. For instance, persons who eat a particular diet that consists of foods they would not ordinarily eat, then quickly put on weight (or, more accurately, fat) soon after quitting the diet, will often give up on their desire to take off pounds. Similarly, exercisers who do not experience rapid success, that is, meet goals quickly, will presume that the task is of insurmountable difficulty and quit exercising, perhaps due to low self-efficacy (Lox et al., 2003).

McAuley and Mihalko (1998) reviewed over 100 studies on the effects of self-efficacy theory on exercise behavior. They concluded that self-efficacy more strongly predicts exercise participation and maintenance if the individual: (a) selects the type of exercise behavior undertaken, a concept called *perceived choice*, (b) possesses certain *thought patterns*, such as optimism, positive arousal, low anxiety, and intrinsic motivation (i.e., exercising for pleasure and enjoyment, high self-determination and competence), (c) *expends optimal effort* and feels capable of redoubling efforts in the face of barriers and challenges, and (d) has *reasonably high expectations* of successful performance and desirable outcomes. To McAuley and Mihalko, the strongest influence of self-efficacy on exercise behavior is performance accomplishments. Mastering tasks perceived by the performer as moderate to very difficult markedly increases self-efficacy.

Not surprisingly, one weakness of self-efficacy theory, acknowledged by the authors, is that even when self-efficacy beliefs about exercise are high, "the decision to embark on an exercise program . . . is fraught with challenges especially when individuals are sedentary, older, or recovering from a life-threatening disease" (McAuley & Mihalko, p. 372). Engaging in physical activity at the correct level of intensity, duration, and frequency to obtain sufficient health and medical benefits is simply too unpleasant for some individuals, particularly if they live a sedentary lifestyle. Thus, the "benefits" of remaining sedentary and not exercising (e.g., having more time to do other things, not experiencing the discomfort associated with vigorous exercise) are greater than the "costs" of remaining sedentary (e.g., weight gain, poorer health, shortened lifespan).

Transtheoretical Model

Perhaps changing behavior from sedentary to active, rather than consisting of one determinant, consists of a series of stages, as suggested in Prochaska and DiClemente's (1983) transtheoretical model. Their model was originally applied to addictive behaviors and later modified to exercise by Prochaska and Marcus (1994).

According to the transtheoretical model, the decision to begin and maintain a habit of exercise, not unlike many behavior changes, occurs over a long period of time. Since the decision to change one's behavior is not always permanent, such as attempts at dieting, or cessation from smoking, the model is cyclical, not linear. Behavioral patterns occur repeatedly in five stages.

Precontemplation

At this stage, for the next six months the inactive person has no intention of exercising. Reasons include no perceived need to exercise, unpleasant experiences with previous attempts at exercising, social pressures not to exercise (e.g., lack of approval from family and friends, self-consciousness about exercising in a public facility in the presence of fitter, younger individuals), not being able to afford exercise equipment or fitness club memberships, or living too far away from available programs and facilities.

Contemplation

At this stage, the person now intends to start exercising within the next 6 months, and may become enlightened about the advantages of exercise through written materials, advice from a physician, or at the urging of friends or family members. The "costs" of not exercising are now beginning to become excessive and the benefits are increasingly more attractive. Prochaska and Marcus (1994) report that "on the average, individuals stay in this relatively stable stage for at least 2 years, telling themselves that someday they will change but putting off change" (p. 162). These individuals are called *chronic contemplators*.

Preparation

At this stage, there is the intention to start exercising "in the near future," usually within a month. Typically, an action plan is formulated, although the plan may not be carried out to obtain the optimal benefits (e.g., exercising only on the weekend rather than at least 3 times a week). Finally, the individual is not yet fully committed to the plan because the disadvantages of exercising (e.g., not enough time, cost of a fitness club membership, lack of space for exercise equipment in the house, physical discomfort) still outweigh the advantages.

Action

The person has finally initiated an exercise routine—for less than 6 months. While the person now exerts extensive energy in implementing an exercise regimen, Prochaska and Marcus (1994) claim, "it is the least stable stage and tends to correspond with the highest risk for relapse" (p. 163). This stage endures for about 6 months. One uncertainty about this stage concerns the criteria that constitute action. Unknown is whether "action" means exercising 3 times per week at a given intensity and duration, or that it represents any consistent and enduring change in exercise behavior. As Prochaska and Marcus (1994) conclude, "problems exist in areas for which there is no agreed upon criteria" (p. 163).

Maintenance

After a period of 6 months, there is now less risk that the person will quit the new behavior. Similar to the action stage, there is uncertainty in the literature about the operational definition of maintenance. Writers in the behavioral medicine literature (e.g., Rand & Weeks, 1998) have used terms such as *partial adherence, ideal adherence, appropriate adherence, erratic adherence*, and *involuntary adherence* to reflect the criterion under which the behavioral change was originally intended, planned, and would result in the desired (anticipated) outcome. Thus, exercising once per week instead of the planned or prescribed three times per week reflect partial adherence. Five years of maintaining an exercise habit is the time interval in which a person will not return to their previous, nonexercise lifestyle.

Termination

At this stage, there is no temptation to engage in the old behavior and 100% confidence to overcome previously tempting situations. A review of the addiction literature, however, where the transtheoretical model was derived, reveals that reverting to previous habits is always possible. Exercise cessation is more likely under conditions such as high demands on time, injury, one or more unpleasant exercise-related experience, poor weather, breakage or loss of equipment, or other, more tempting, activities that replace exercise. The absence of other factors also contribute to dropping the exercise habit such as lack of social support, failure to meet goals, increased exercise difficulty due to weight gain or aging, or lack of financial resources to afford a fitness club membership.

The transtheoretical model, as applied to exercise behavior, has serious limitations, however. For example, Bandura (1997) expresses concerns that the model fails to reflect fundamental tenets of traditional stage theory, while Rosen's (2000) meta-analysis indicated that readiness for exercise may not be a discrete (i.e., yes-no) variable but a continuous variable (i.e., not at all—very little—somewhat—very much—extremely). In addition, to test the model's efficacy requires providing individuals with intervention strategies that are compatible with their particular exercise stage, and then measure their exercise behavior over a prolonged period of time, perhaps several years. Finally, in their review and critique of the model, Buckworth and Dishman (2002) concluded:

> The usefulness of the transtheoretical model for exercise interventions has been mixed. Targeting specific processes of change to facilitate progression of exercise behavior across stages is based on the assumption that differences between adjacent stages found in cross-sectional studies point to processes that need to be changed to progress to the next stage. However, the efficacy of targeting specific processes to promote stage progression has

yet to be adequately tested; there have been few longitudinal prospective designs, and the instruments to measure stage and processes of changes have been poorly validated for exercise. (p. 223)

RELAPSE PREVENTION MODEL

This model addresses self-controlled efforts needed to maintain exercise behavior and to adapt responsibly to situations that promote former, undesirable behavior patterns. The model was originally created by Marlatt and Gordon (1985) to promote abstinence from engaging frequently in addictive behaviors. The individual is taught to use cognitive and behavioral strategies in dealing productively with relapses in desirable behaviors, in this case, exercise.

Conceptually, the relapse prevention model is appealing when addressing exercise behavior, in general, and adherence, in particular. Exercise relapse is clearly a significant problem, and any approach to minimize this process is needed. However, as pointed out by Buckworth and Dishman (2002), "the model was developed for maintaining cessation of high-frequency undesired behaviors, and exercise is a low-frequency, desired behavior" (p. 225). The authors contend it is difficult to detect an exercise lapse or to deal with a lapse in time to forestall relapse. Along these lines, the model does not account for overcoming an *adherence violation effect*, in which missing one or more exercise sessions permanently abandons future exercise habits. Factors such as lifestyle imbalances and prioritizing self-gratification (e.g., leading a sedentary lifestyle) over devotion and energy toward more health-enhancing activities, are not overcome by this model. Thus, while this model provides valuable insights into strategies for promoting exercise adherence, it lacks the incentives and emotions needed to overcome the "benefits" of committing to regular exercise.

Deterrence Theory

While unintended for exercise behavior, deterrence theory (Paternoster, 1987) posits that a person contemplates committing a crime by weighing the costs and benefits of this illegal action. If the punishment for the act is highly certain and severe, and it outweighs the perceived benefits of the act, the person is more likely to conclude it is not in his or her best interests to commit the act and then avoids it. On the other hand, if the perceived benefits outweigh the costs, the crime act becomes more desirable and is more likely to be executed. It is the subjective perception of the individual rather than the objective reality of legal sanctions that determines future behavior. Although deterrence theory has not been examined with respect to exercise behavior, it is reasonable to surmise that a person is more likely to engage in regular exercise if the harmful effects of inactivity are perceived as certain and severe. Perhaps the link between deterrence theory and exercise is more closely evident in Strelan and Boeckmann's (2003) Drugs in Sport Deterrence Model.

Drugs in Sport Deterrence Model (DSDM)

Strelan and Boeckmann (2003) have applied deterrence theory within the context of athletes' use of banned substances in their DSDM. One assumption of deterrence theory is that individuals make conscious decisions based on extensive information, planning, and justification to optimize the decision-maker's best interests. This assumption holds true for an athlete's decision to use performance-enhancing drugs. The athlete's dilemma is to weigh the benefits of drug use (e.g., improved performance, recognition and glory, meeting the expectations of others, high income from sponsorships, personal satisfaction) against the possible costs (e.g., a ban from future competition, poor health over the long term, reduced income, future possible success, ostracism by peers and the public, loss of respect from significant others).

Situational factors also influence behavioral predictions of the cost-benefit trade-off. For example, the sport culture, including peers, teammates, and coaches, may encourage or discourage drug use. Legal sanctions, as well as current policies of the sport organization and team, are other situational factors. The drug's availability, their financial cost, and evidence of monitoring, or drug testing, are yet additional considerations that influence drug use.

The DSDM adequately describes the importance of a person's perceptions of the benefits and costs of certain behaviors, such as exercise, that are inherently undesirable, illegal, or immoral. The cost-benefit tradeoffs are salient, all of which are mediated by situational factors. The DSDM, however, is a conceptual model not an intervention model, that, at best, describes the factors that underlie drug-taking behavior. Similar factors can be used to describe exercise behavior in which the person determines the benefits and costs of exercising, as opposed to leading a sedentary lifestyle.

Overview of Limitations of Health Behavior Models and Theories

There is one problem associated with all of these models that researchers have not addressed—at least not consistently. How does the public define exercise? Ask individuals who walk a mile a day if they exercise, and they say "yes." Others will categorize themselves as exercisers if they lift weights or engage in flexibility exercises. However, the general mental and physical health benefits of exercise are minimal unless a person engages in *aerobic* exercise. The validity of theories and models in explaining and predicting exercise behavior is clouded by the failure to recognize what *type* of exercise, and the frequency and intensity with which it is performed, we are trying to encourage. Perhaps it's best to simply encourage people, especially if they are elderly, overweight, or recovering from sickness or injury, to engage in *any* type of physical activity habit they view as possible, safe, desirable, and mentally stimulating. If our standards for exercise participation consist of reaching our target heart rate or engaging in aerobic exercise at the exclusion of other forms of exercise, we—researchers, writers, and practitioners—might be setting the bar too high and actually inhibiting a more active lifestyle in our society.

Evidence exists that, to some degree, each of these models and theories explain or predict behavior. One inherent limitation of these models, however, is the absence of examining the role of a person's *values* in determining future behavior. Strelan and Boeckmann (2003) acknowledge the importance of morality as a powerful deterrent to inappropriate behavior, yet neglect to add this factor to their model. As Haan, Aerts, and Cooper (1985) recognize, individuals are more likely to adhere to a particular belief if it is ingrained early and often in life. Values about the importance of developing exercise habits as a lifelong habit has been missing heretofore in the extant exercise psychology intervention literature. Chapter 10 describes a values-based intervention model that helps the individual identify the disconnect between their negative habit of nonexercise and their values such as health, family, performance excellence, and other positive outcomes related to a long-term commitment to exercise.

Chapter 4

Mental Health Benefits of Exercise

The physiological and health benefits of exercise have been well known by researchers, educators, and the public for many years. Less well known, however, are the psychological—cognitive and emotional—benefits of exercise. Psychological outcomes from engaging in exercise have been studied in both acute (i.e., a single exercise bout) and chronic forms (i.e., over a period of weeks and months). It is equally important to acknowledge *all* exercise benefits—short-term and long-term—because physical activity is a valid and reliable form of treatment to enhance mental health. Exercise is known to effectively manage stress, anxiety, depression, and other undesirable mood states. However, these benefits accrue after several weeks and months (Berger et al., 2002; Buckworth & Dishman, 2002).

This chapter will provide a brief overview of the literature on how *personality traits* may predict exercise participation, and the effects of exercise on *self-esteem*, *stress*, *acute* and *chronic anxiety*, and *mood state*—something the MHP needs to know in prescribing exercise to clients.

PERSONALITY

While an overview of personality theory goes well beyond the scope of this chapter, it is suffice to say that the link between exercise and personality is not about cause and effect. That is, exercise cannot change personality. Personality is a relatively stable structure that is shaped by a person's actions and reactions to his or her environment. To use Hollander's (1967) well-known personality structure, personality has been divided into three components: the *personality core*, *typical responses*, and *role-related behaviors*. The personality core is developed from early environmental interactions and is a reflection of who we are. It includes our perceptions of self and the external world, our attitudes, values, interests, motives, and self-concept (the latter of which is reviewed separately in this chapter). The core is not susceptible to change through behaviors, such as exercise. Typical responses consist of our somewhat predictable behaviors and the ways in which we react to our environment. Thus, a withdrawn person will not likely feel comfortable in a new environment such as an exercise facility without onsite social support, such as exercising with a friend or establishing good rapport with fitness staff.

Role-related behaviors consist of more variable, daily behaviors influenced by the particular context in which they function. Thus, a person who is withdrawn in social settings might be relatively assertive in the setting of his or her business or even aggressive as a competitive athlete. In summary, then, the core is least likely to change, while role-related behaviors are most changeable from exercise participation. It is the latter dimension that warrants examination of the effects of exercise on personality.

Type A Behavior Pattern

Type A behavior pattern, which was originally—and erroneously—called a personality trait (e.g., coronary-prone personality) reflects the person's tendency to exhibit assertiveness, anger, hostility, time urgency, impatience, and susceptibility to stress and anxiety. In their brief review of this literature, Lox et al. (2003) have concluded that involvement in a chronic exercise program (e.g., a minimum of 8–12 weeks) will reduce cardiovascular reactivity to psychosocial stress. However, the authors also report that type A's have lower adherence rates to exercise programs—perhaps because of their impatience with obtaining their exercise goals—and have higher rates of exercise-related injuries than do type B's. On a positive note, type A's exert greater effort during exercise, causing a greater physiological response during exercise.

Hardiness

Hardiness is defined as the tendency to involve oneself in life's experiences rather than to be alienated or threatened by them or to passively observe them (Kobasa, 1979). Examples include taking personal control of life's events, becoming task involved and focused, engaging in aerobic exercise, seeking social support systems, and having a sense of humor. Hardiness moderates the deleterious effects of life stress on physical and mental health, and is positively associated with engaging in regular exercise. Unknown, and less likely, however, is whether exercise participation actually promotes hardiness tendencies.

Selected Personality Traits

The effects of exercise on an array of personality traits have been studied over the years, particularly in the 1960's and 1970's. Not surprisingly, the results of these studies have been mixed. In his extensive review, Leith (1994) found scant evidence of an exercise-personality link. Reasons abound including the stable, long-term nature of personality traits, the prolonged time period needed to change personality, and the vast array of exercise characteristics (e.g., type, intensity, duration per bout, improved fitness) that are difficult to control in explaining a cause and effect relationship. However, exercise has been far more effective in favorably changing cognition such as attentional focusing, concentration, and memory and affective disorders (e.g., clinical anxiety, depression, bipolar illness). In a comprehensive review of the exercise and mental health literature back in 1981, Folkins and Sime concluded that exercise leads to improved mood, self-concept, work behavior, and cognitive functioning during and soon following an exercise bout. However, with the exception of self-concept, personality is unaffected by improvements in physical fitness. Thus, personality cannot be "treated" by engaging in an exercise program, however, exercise markedly influences psychopathology, which will be discussed later.

SELF-ESTEEM

Some authors consider self-esteem a personality trait, while others view it as dispositional and susceptible to change. *Self-esteem*, highly similar in meaning to a concept called *self-worth*, is typically defined as the degree to which individuals like or approve of themselves. These concepts are multidimensional, meaning that there are different sources of self-esteem. These include knowledge (academic) self-esteem, physical/somatic self-esteem, sport self-esteem, social self-esteem, religious self-esteem, family self-esteem, and work self-esteem. Buckworth and Dishman (2002) describe self-esteem as a function of physical self-worth, with subdimensions of sport, physical condition, body, and strength. Does exercise alter any of the dimensions of self-esteem, especially given the fact that is it a relatively stable, long-term disposition? Buckworth and Dishman's extensive review of the literature concluded that "positive associations between exercise and self-esteem have been found, but effects are stronger for individuals initially lower in self-esteem," and that "exercise has more potent effects on physical self-concept and self-esteem than on general self-perceptions" (p. 168). The authors also found that, among females, exercise is especially tied to body/physique self-esteem. Concomitant changes in other forms of self-esteem (e.g., family, academic, sport) were not noted.

In summary, any behavior such as exercise that induces a sense of competence and achievement, and that is perceived as enjoyable and produces desirable changes in a person's physical characteristics (e.g., weight/fat loss, increased strength), will positively influence self-esteem, particularly in the physical dimension. Although other dimensions of self-esteem, such as academic, work, family, and so on, do not seem to be affected similarly, as Buckworth and Dishman conclude, "positive self-esteem is associated with good mental health, so linking exercise with improvement in physical self-concept and thus with better self-esteem offers another reason for adopting and maintaining a physically active lifestyle" (p. 174).

STRESS AND ANXIETY

To clarify, as MHPs would know, stress and anxiety are not the same thing. Psychosocial stress, as opposed to biological forms of stress (e.g., pain, intense physical activity) is typically viewed as a mental state based on a current perception of immediate threat or harm. Stress reflects a person's sense of immediate danger. It can be either "good" (e.g., laughter, excitement) or "bad" (e.g., tension, anger).

Anxiety, on the other hand, reflects an individual's perceptions of worry, apprehension, and threat about a *future* event. It is always a *negative* emotion or mood state. Anxiety is categorized as *trait*, defined as a feature of personality in which an individual is predisposed to perceive apparently harmless situations as threatening, or *state*, defined as an immediate emotional state to perceive an approaching situation as threatening.

In addition, there exists both acute (short-term) anxiety and chronic (long-term) forms of anxiety. *Aerobic* exercise has a favorable influence on both acute and chronic anxiety. Exercise benefits only state, not trait, anxiety, however. Stress and anxiety have both physiological (e.g., heart rate, blood pressure, muscular tension) and cognitive components (described earlier).

Acute exercise involves single bouts of exercise at some level of intensity or duration. Chronic exercise, on the other hand, typically involves a program, performed either in a group or alone condition, in a formal exercise facility or at home, for a period of weeks or months designed to improve aerobic capacity. However, engaging in resistance (strength) conditioning also has numerous health advantages and is recommended (Anshel et al., 2003).

Exercise and Stress

How does exercise affect stress? Their extensive review of the related literature, Buckworth and Dishman (2002) concluded "aerobic exercise programs lasting at least a few months seem best for reducing reports of chronic stress" (p. 79). The mechanisms by which this positive effect occurs seems to be the short-term distraction from unpleasant thoughts and/or increasing feelings of control or commitment that buffers the impact of stressful events. Stress-reducing properties are more likely if each exercise session lasts for at least 30 minutes (Leith, 1998).

Another line of research has focused on the effects of aerobic exercise on a person's reaction to stress, called *stress reactivity*. Results of a review by Crews and Landers (1987) indicated a moderate effect for fitness on stress reactivity with fitter individual showing less (i.e., superior) reactivity. Stronger effects were shown after acute (i.e., a single bout) exercise rather than chronic (i.e., over a period of weeks or months) involvement in exercise. It appears, then, that exercise will improve a person's ability to react to sudden stress.

Exercise and Anxiety

The finding in numerous research studies, reviewed by Petruzzello and his colleagues (1991), is that even a single bout of aerobic exercise, as well as involvement in a longer-term aerobic exercise program, will markedly reduce state anxiety. Aerobic exercise has also benefited patients with various anxiety disorders (e.g., panic disorder, post-traumatic stress disorder) and clinical depression. These findings were similar for individuals with varying levels of initial fitness level. A review of this literature by Biddle and Mutrie (2001) indicated that exercise is associated with a significant small-to-moderate reduction in anxiety. This holds true for both acute and chronic exercise, state and trait anxiety, and for both genders.

Exercise of any type, however, is not likely to influence trait anxiety because of its permanent, unchanging nature. As indicated earlier, personality traits, such as trait anxiety, are simply not susceptible to short-term treatments. Reasons for the positive effects of exercise on state anxiety include favorable changes in the exerciser's biochemistry, "time-out," or distraction, from the sources or symptoms of anxiety, heightened sense of competence and achievement, improved self-concept, and increased social support (see Buckworth & Dishman, 2002, for a review of this literature).

NEGATIVE AFFECT (MOOD)

Mood is usually measured as a state characteristic. Therefore, research on the effects of exercise on mood have focused on immediate, rather than long-term, effects. Berger and Motl (2000) conducted perhaps the most recent and comprehensive review of the research literature related to the effects of exercise on mood. The authors examined studies over the past 25 years in which mood was measured specifically by the Profile of Mood States (POMS). They concluded that there is unequivocal support for the mood-enhancing effects of exercise, specifically on improved vigor and reduced tension, depression, anger, confusion, and fatigue. The authors attribute changes in mood following exercise to psychological mechanisms, including "enhanced self-concept, feelings of self-efficacy, enjoyment, expectancy of psychological benefits, 'time out' from one's routine and daily hassles, and an increased sense of control" (p. 84).

Physiological mechanisms (e.g., cortisol, endorphins, monoamines), reflecting biochemical changes, may also partly explain mood alteration during and after exercise. With respect to exercise intensity, the authors recommend that unless a participant prefers low or high exercise intensity, optimal conditions for mood changes occur at a moderate intensity level. Moderate intensity exercise, particularly aerobic exercise, has been repeatedly shown to reduce negative mood and improves positive mood state.

DEPRESSION

As any MHP knows, "depression falls under a category of mental disorders that the *Diagnostic and Statistical Manual of Mental Disorders* classifies as 'mood disturbances' and includes disorders that influence mood regulation beyond the usual variations between sadness and happiness/excitement" (Lox et al., 2003, p. 132). Because exercise has been shown to reduce symptoms of depression, it is important to describe its characteristics:

- sustained feelings of sadness or elation;
- feelings of guilt or worthlessness
- disturbances in appetite
- disturbances in sleep patterns
- lack of energy
- difficulty concentrating
- loss of interest in all or most activities
- problems with memory
- thoughts of suicide
- hallucinations

The effects of exercise on depression have been studied since the 1960s. The research has taken primarily two forms, exercise as a preventive measure of depression and effects of exercise on existing depression. Extensive reviews of literature conducted by Lox et al. (2003), Buckworth and Dishman (2002), and Biddle and Mutrie (2001) have shown extensive benefits of exercise on both depression prevention and remedy. In a recent study, Dunn, Trivedi, Kampert, Clark, and Chambliss (2005) found that aerobic exercise significantly decreased depression among clinically depressed patients as opposed to a placebo group.

Preventive Effects

Several studies have shown depression prevention effects. Lox et al. reported the following results:

- Women who were sedentary or engaged in little activity were twice as likely to develop depression over an eight-year follow-up period as compared to those who were at least moderately active;

- There is an association between inactivity and incidence of depression between 1965 and 1983. The risk of developing depression was significantly greater for men and women at both follow-up periods (1974–1983) if they were inactive in 1965.

- Physical activity at baseline was negatively associated with depression 25 years later, that is, more activity predicted lower depression.

- Among a sample of 2,084 older males and females who reported greater numbers of depressive symptoms at baseline, those who subsequently became daily walkers had a higher likelihood of reduced depressive symptoms at the 3-year follow-up.

- Men in their 20s who engaged in 3 or more hours of sport activity per week at baseline had a 27% reduction in the likelihood of developing depression at follow-up compared to those who played for less than 1 hour per week.

• Physically inactive people are over three times more likely to have depression than those who engage in regular physical activity.

Exercise as Treatment

Can exercise be useful as a behavioral strategy to combat depression?

• In a meta-analysis of 80 studies, North, McCullagh, and Tran (1990) found: (a) exercise resulted in decreased depression, (b) some factors moderated exercise treatment effects more than others, (c) exercise was as or more effective than traditional therapies, and (d) all types of exercise similarly reduced depression. Weight training, aerobic activity, and walking all had similar effects on depression.

• The length of the exercise program is not as important as simply engaging in the activity. Studies in which exercise interventions ranged from 4 to 24 weeks revealed no significant differences in depression.

• Exercise helped decrease depression for all age groups and genders.

• Initial level of depression was not important concerning level of depression reduction following exercise.

• Exercise intensity was a factor in reduced depression. Individuals who trained harder experienced a greater reduction in depression.

• Exercising was as effective as a depression-reducing treatment as using pharmacotherapy alone or the combination of pharmacotherapy and exercise.

• Exercise will improve clinical depression if exercise training: (a) occurs at least over a period of five weeks, (b) is performed at least three times per week of aerobic or nonaerobic, (c) is of low to moderate intensity level (50% of predicted maximum heart rate), and (d) occurs over 20 to 60 minutes in duration.

EXERCISE RECOMMENDATIONS
FOR PROMOTING POSITIVE AFFECT

The MHP is in a position to foster pleasant exercise experiences and positive emotions, as well as to reduce depression, anxiety, other forms of psychopathology, and undesirable mood states. These examples serve the objective of giving the client a feeling of security, which will more likely lead to positive emotional outcomes from their exercise experience (see Leith, 1998, for additional information in this area).

Perceived Choice of Exercise

It is important that clients select the type of exercise in which they wish to participate. Lox et al. (2003) recommend information about the individual's past experiences with exercise should be obtained to determine which activities they have found enjoyable. Begin by choosing moderate-intensity activities you enjoy the most. By choosing activities they enjoy, they'll be more likely to stick with them. It is also important, however, that they include aerobic-type exercise to obtain the optimal mental and physical health benefits. For instance, they can choose to engage in brisk walking or jogging on their own, or join an exercise class. Clients should also participate in resistance training for reasons presented in chapter 6.

Goals, if Used, Should Be Achievable; Moderate at Best

This writer feels that goal setting is overstated as an important motivator in sport and exercise. First, setting a performance goal that is both achievable and challenging is needed to make it motivating, but it is very difficult, especially in exercise. Second, if a person derives satisfaction from mere participation in any activity, then why is it so important to attach a goal to it? Of course, some individuals find goals motivating and they tend to reflect competence and achievement when a standard is met. However, goals can also translate into failure if the exerciser does not meet the goal.

Adapt to the Person's Lifestyle

It is possible to prescribe exercises that blend in with the client's daily routines, such as walking to work, taking frequent recovery breaks during the day by walking stairs or some other physical activity, engaging in household activities, taking up recreational activities such as bicycling, hiking, or gardening, or purchasing equipment that has motivational value such as a pedometer, treadmill, or heart rate monitor.

Exercises Should Be Fail-Safe

The last thing a novice exerciser needs is to feel he or she has failed to meet self-expectations or the expectations of others. Exercise experiences should be nonjudgmental, and exercisers should not feel they have failed to meet standards. At the same time, exercisers, from novices through more advanced, need to feel challenged to improve their fitness level. Cardiovascular fitness can only be achieved by increasing heart rate over a period of 20 to 30 minutes. How to accomplish this challenging task is discussed in chapter 6.

Gradually Increase Intensity

It has taken years for your client to become overweight and out of shape. It will take time—perhaps 6–8 weeks—to feel a marked improvement in fitness, although initial improvement can be detected in only 4 weeks. Your client should gradually build up time spent doing the activity by adding a few minutes every week or two until he or she can comfortably perform a minimum of 30 minutes per day. As the minimum amount becomes easier, a gradual increase of either the length of time performing an activity or increasing the intensity of the activity—or both—is recommended.

Ensure Social Support

Most novices want to exercise with a friend or establish good rapport with fitness center staff. The MHP might try to introduce a client to other participants or encourage the client to attend a fitness center with a friend, partner, or spouse. An MHP who already exercises might even consider attending the exercise venue with their client, at least initially to get them comfortable with the facility, program, and exercise task (Lox et al., 2003). One other source of social support is to involve family members to either encourage the client to exercise regularly, to purchase and use fitness equipment in the home and to exercise with the client, or to escort the client to a fitness facility (hopefully, to exercise along with the client).

Keep the Environment Comfortable and Secure

It is important that clients feel comfortable in the fitness environment. This can take two forms. Externally, clients should be able to walk from their car to the facility without feelings of intimidation or having safety concerns. Second, the client should also feel comfortable inside the exercise facility and with staff. They should feel free to ask questions, be able to try out an exercise class to see if they want to return without the obligation to register for it, and feel welcomed, in general.

Use Baseline Measures

Data often drive behavior. Clients should have fitness tests that serve as baseline measures against which to compare and determine progress. Examples of such tests include blood work (e.g., cholesterol, triglycerides), submaximal oxygen uptake VO^2 test to measure cardiovascular fitness, strength testing, percent body fat, blood pressure, and flexibility measures.

Ensure Performance Coaching

This is particularly important to ensure proper exercise technique, testing of initial fitness level, and motivation to persist on task. As in any other profession, performance coaches vary in their knowledge, communication skills, interests in helping clients, and personal qualities. They earn a salary to carry out their responsibility, so it is imperative that clients feel comfortable with their coach. The length of time a coach works with clients varies, however, there should be sufficient time to provide instruction, testing, and measuring progress. Many coaches remain with their clients for months; about 4–6 weeks is the norm until the client can exercise on his or her own without additional instruction, feedback, and motivation.

Going at Your Own Pace

It is challenging enough to actually attend a fitness facility or begin an exercise program. The challenge is far greater if novice exercisers are asked to "keep up" with an instructor or with the expectations of others. The key goal of getting started is to develop an exercise routine certain days of the week and hours of the day. The level of intensity and duration is less important in the initial phases. Therefore, it is imperative that clients do not feel pressure to "keep up" with instructors, with other group members, or with anyone else in which they are being judged. Later, once the exercise routine has been established, clients can begin increasing the challenge (e.g., intensity and duration) of their exercise session.

Pre-Exercise Rituals

The self-monitoring checklist (Appendix A) includes specific guidelines for engaging in certain thoughts and behaviors the day of and immediately before exercise sessions. These should be learned and practiced until they become automatic because the goal of these strategies is to foster a more enjoyable, less stressful and more efficient exercise session. Examples of pre-exercise rituals include drinking enough water, using positive self-talk (e.g., "I can do this" or "I'm ready—lets go!"), avoid eating, caffeine, or smoking within 1–2 hours before exercising, and perceiving the coming session as enjoyable or challenging, not as threatening or unpleasant.

Recognize Setbacks

Help clients understand that setbacks—called relapses—may occur and to devise strategies to prevent these relapses from becoming permanent. Illness, injury or discomfort, expense of a club membership, loss of social support, lack of progress, not meeting goals, and chronic stress can each lead to loss of motivation to exercise.

MECHANISMS OF CHANGE

While behavioral studies have shown the psychological benefits of exercise on mental illness and mood, the underlying reasons that explain these effects are less certain. Here are the prevailing theories and explanations as reviewed by Fox et al. (2003), and Biddle and Mutrie (2001).

Anthropological Hypothesis

Following an evolutionary perspective, it is thought the physical activity is a natural part of human existence. Our species was—and remains, in many cultures—hunter-gatherers, and has been traditionally physically active (e.g., manual labor, manual transportation, sport), at least until relatively recently in our history. There has been a significant relationship between the rate at which we became more sedentary and the rate of depression. Depression has increased dramatically in the U.S., accompanied by lower rates of exercise and other forms of physical activity. In addition, more physically active cultures, such as in Scandinavian countries, suffer from lower rates of depression than in the U.S. The anthropological hypothesis suggests that human beings are genetically predisposed to be physically active.

Endorphin Hypothesis

Endorphins are neuropeptides that cause "neurons to "communicate." Endorphins are the body's own natural painkillers. If, for example, endorphins are released during exercise and exercise makes us feel less depressed, then the increased endorphins could be the reason why. It is thought, then, that changes in our biochemistry explains why exercise makes us feel better (i.e., less depressed and anxious).

Serotonin and Norepinephrine Hypotheses

These hypotheses are reported together because they are both monomines; they alter brain neurotransmitters and alter emotion. It is thought that exercise can increase the rate at which neurotransmitters are produced, or released into the spaces between neurons, thereby facilitating between-neuron communication. The reduced is elevated mood state. Evidence of this explanation for linking exercise with reduced depression is based solely on animal research.

Mastery/Physical Self-Efficacy Hypotheses

It is thought that exercise creates a sense of accomplishment, competence, or mastery upon completing challenging tasks (e.g., improved strength or endurance performance). Improved intrinsic motivation, self-worth, and personal control are likely outcomes. Behavioral mastery also enhances self-concept/self-esteem. Physical self-efficacy refers to a person's sense of perceived competence, skill mastery, and improved physical stature or accomplishments (e.g., physical performance, musculature, reduced body fat/bodyweight) due to physical effort. For this reason, clients should have quantitative indicators of success during their exercise regimen.

Social Interaction Hypothesis

Many, though not all, individuals enjoy exercising in the company of others (e.g., taking an exercise class, jogging with a friend, visiting a fitness center). It is proposed that exercise reduces depression because it provides an opportunity for the exerciser to interact with others. Of course, many individuals prefer to exercise alone and still feel very positive feelings as a result. Speaking anecdotally, my experience consulting with patients in cardiac and pulmonary exercise rehabilitation settings clearly indicates a strong social incentive for exercise adherence. Patients have often told me of their reliance on meeting peers at the exercise venue as an important incentive to remain active in the exercise program. Given the high rate of depression among these patients, the social interaction hypothesis appears plausible. Thus, for many individuals, exercise offers an opportunity to socially interact with others, a source of life satisfaction.

Distraction/Time-Out Hypothesis

Exercise provides an opportunity to "tune out" sources of stress and other unpleasant thoughts and emotions, which are sources of depression and anxiety. The exerciser, then, is mentally "occupied" with the task at hand—exercise—which requires full concentration and relaxation. This is why exercisers should not have their cell phones in the exercise venue nor should they discuss work while exercising. They are missing an important exercise benefit—escape from the "storms" of life.

STRATEGIES FOR MAKING PHYSICAL ACTIVITY A PART OF DAILY RITUALS

The Centers for Disease Control website, www.cdc.gov, offers the following advice for ensuring rituals of keeping physically active.

1. Walk, cycle, jog, or skate to as many destinations as possible.

2. Park the car further away from your destination.

3. Get on or off the bus, and other forms of public transportation, a few blocks away from your destination.

4. Take the stairs instead of the elevator or escalator.

5. Become active with children or pets.

6. Take fitness breaks. Walk or do desk exercises instead of taking cigarette or coffee breaks.

7. Perform gardening or do home repairs.

8. Use leg power—take small trips on foot to get your body moving.

9. Exercise while watching TV (e.g., use hand weights, stationary bicycle, treadmill).

10. Dance to music.

One should keep a pair of comfortable walking or running shoes in the car and office to be ready for activity whenever the opportunity arises.

Chapter 5

Strategies for Promoting Exercise Motivation

The late comedian, Milton Berle, would joke, "The doctor said (exercise) would add 10 years to my life, and he was right. I feel 10 years older already" (*Orlando Sentinel*, 2002, p. C2). Even individuals who choose to lead a sedentary lifestyle know the benefits of exercise. Yet, they do not exercise, which is contrary to the health belief model. The reasons individuals make the choice to engage in regular exercise while others choose not to exercise, why individuals stop their exercise program, and the factors that contribute to individual differences in the intensity and duration of a single exercise bout are important areas of research in exercise psychology. These issues address the very popular area of *motivation*, a psychological factor that drives a person's thoughts and behaviors.

DEFINING EXERCISE MOTIVATION

Before we explore ways to motivate clients to exercise, it is important to understand the concept of motivation, and how it is defined. The term motivation comes from the Latin word *movere*, meaning "to move." The most popular and inclusive definition of motivation is the tendency for the *direction and selectivity of behavior* to be *controlled by its connections to consequences*, and the tendency of this behavior to *persist until a goal is achieved*. Let's go beyond mere words and examine some important aspects of this definition for exercise. Understanding the components of motivation helps give this concept "life" with respect to helping clients start and maintain a fitness program.

Direction of motivation refers to the purpose and the desired actions of the activity. The motivated exerciser feels compelled to engage in a task that is both purposeful and meaningful. This is why it is important to understand a client's motives to start an exercise program, an issue addressed in the next section. Unless the "exercise habit" has a perceived purpose and benefits, long-term persistence will be unlikely. *Selectivity of behavior* refers to determining the specific exercise task(s) needed to be performed to meet personal needs and goals. The third component of this definition is that behaviors must be *controlled by their connections to consequences*. For example, if a client feels that missing a day or week of exercise is "no big deal," he or she has not linked exercise to specific, meaningful goals; the client does not consider the consequences of not exercising as important or meaningful. Therefore, the person should perceive that *not* exercising, that is, failing to carry out a planned exercise session or series of sessions, carries a cost that is undesirable.

The fourth and final component of motivation is that *desirable behavior should persist until a goal is achieved*. The purpose of exercise motivation is to help a person prolong desirable feelings and actions for as long as possible—at least until meeting a goal. In the case of exercise, however, we are talking about developing and sustaining a lifelong habit. The goals derived from exercise participation can be negative or positive; both have long-term implications. *Negative* exercise goals include avoiding unhealthy conditions such as being overweight or obese, heart disease, and social isolation (i.e., exercise helps fulfill the need for socializing with others). *Positive* exercise goals, on the other hand, include improving physique, mood state, and general health, feeling better about oneself (i.e., heightened confidence and self-esteem), improving various measures of physical fitness, and improved mental and emotional status. Numerous studies unrelated to exercise have shown that positive goals result in more long-term success and adherence to the task than negative goals. Although further research is needed to determine if this remains true in exercise settings, it is plausible to surmise that positive goals are less threatening and more likely to be reached by having motivational properties than negative goals.

There are many forms and sources of motivation, some more attainable than others. While an extensive review of this area goes beyond the purpose of this chapter, it is important to understand the different types of motivation so that MHPs can tap into as many of these with clients as possible. Each of these has implications for working with clients in mental health settings.

Forms of Motivation

Competence Motivation

According to White (1959), the need for competence is an inherent part of life starting in childhood. We feel pleasure in response to successfully mastering our surroundings. Even children are motivated by mastery, curiosity, challenge, and play. Achieving competence bring feelings of internal pleasure and satisfaction. Thus, competence motivation is the intrinsic need to deal effectively with the environment.

Achievement Motivation

The need to achieve is typically viewed as a personality trait. Central to this theory is that some individuals derive extensive satisfaction from success in achievement activities, although "success" is in the mind of the beholder. High need achievers are characterized by: (a) experiencing more pleasure from success, (b) feel responsible for the outcomes of their own actions, (c) prefer to know about their success or failure almost immediately after performance, and (d) prefer situations that contain some risk about the result. Each individual is responsible for determining his or her own achievement behavior. Thus, some clients will view mere participation in exercise (e.g., taking a slow walk) as meeting their fitness goal, while others will "reach higher" and engage in more strenuous activity.

Intrinsic Motivation (IM)

It is suffice to say that IM, derived primarily from the original work of Deci (1975), is imperative to the long-term commitment to most activities, especially an activity that is strenuous and time-consuming such as exercise. IM reflects a person's actions that are performed voluntarily, without coercion, and that are perceived as pleasant. The words fun, satisfaction, voluntary, fulfilling, self-determining, and competence reflect this form of motivation. A high degree of IM in exercise settings will more likely lead to adherence than low feelings of IM, when behavior is motivated by external sources (discussed next). Conditions that promote IM in exercise settings are: (a) a client's own decision to engage in an exercise program, called self-determination, (b) the client's need to feel competent, (c) a client's perception of control over their environment (hence, the need to be coached or receive social support at an exercise venue), (d) receiving positive information, which promotes feelings of competence, and (e) receiving outcomes from exercise participation that are perceived as satisfying, rewarding, and pleasurable. *The Intrinsic Exerciser* (Houghton Mifflin, 2002), by Dr. J. Kimiecik, is a highly readable book on ways to enhance IM in exercise settings.

Extrinsic Motivation (EM)

Whereas IM is derived from internal sources of competence, satisfaction, fun, and pleasure, EM promotes exercise behavior when: (a) a person receives tangible external rewards, and (b) when the person's primary motive to engage in the activity is dependent on, or determined by, receiving those tangible rewards. Examples include money, awards (e.g., trophies, ribbons, certificates, t-shirts), personal data (e.g., weight loss, reduced body fat), and public recognition and approval. The limitation of EM is that the absence of such externally derived rewards often results in cessation of the activity. Thus, individuals who are exercising for the primary purpose of losing weight, but find that weight loss is nonexistent or minimal after a certain time period is more likely to discontinue their exercise program, as opposed to individuals who exercise for enjoyment and feel satisfaction from the activity as an end in itself.

In summary, your clients will not begin an exercise program, and certainly not persist after starting one, if they lack the proper level and sources of motivation. The first step in the process of promoting client motivation is helping clients understand the importance and benefits of engaging in regular exercise. One approach to this process is provided in chapter 10.

Briefly, the MHP can help clients link their non-exercise habits to their values, helping them identify a disconnect between their values (e.g., health, family, performance excellence) and their negative habits (e.g., not exercising, poor nutrition), to determine the costs and long-term consequences of their negative habits, to conclude whether or not this disconnect is acceptable, especially given the habit's costs and consequences. If the disconnect is acceptable, clients will not change, and a long-term commitment to exercise less likely to occur. If, however, the disconnect is unacceptable, then the client is far more likely to be receptive to an "action plan" in which they create a new exercise routine. This would include an array of cognitive (e.g., positive self-talk, improved confidence and optimism) and behavioral strategies (e.g., obtain a fitness club membership and personal coach, purchase new fitness clothing and shoes, develop new healthier habits) that promote a long-term commitment to exercise.

MOTIVES FOR EXERCISING

Before MHPs can help clients become motivated to exercise, it is important to know the reasons a client would want to develop a new set of rituals to improve fitness. When the MHPs know their client's exercise motives, they can develop cognitive and behavioral strategies to help meet those needs and motives. Based on the Exercise Motivation Scale (Markland & Ingledew, 1997) and suggestions from Lox et al. (2003) and Anshel and Reeves (1998), here are the most common motives for exercising and concomitant strategies that will enable clients to start and maintain their exercise program.

Improved Health

Individuals who start an exercise program are more likely to be motivated by improving their health than any other reason—improved physical appearance, such as weight loss, is ranked second. Areas of improved health include a better lipids profile (e.g., cholesterol, triglycerides, liver and kidney function), lower blood pressure, slower resting heart rate, reduced percent body fat (coupled with increased lean body mass), and improved stress test results. For clients with a strong health motive quantitative data is extremely important. Changes in health status are driven by numbers, that is, favorable changes in test results. The MHP should be sure their clients receive baseline (i.e., before their exercise program) health tests, then obtain test results every 3 to 6 months to detect changes—hopefully improved changes—in these scores.

Enhanced Physical Appearance

Body weight, percent of weight that consists of muscle as opposed to fat, called percent body fat, "fitter" appearance, changes in the way clothing fits, and remarks by others about a client's appearance are all signals of improved physical appearance. Social support is an important strategy to ensure the exerciser is receiving needed positive messages. Sources of this information include the MHP, family members, exercise companions, the client's personal physician, work colleagues, and fitness staff.

Improved Fitness

Similar to the need for improved health, clients whose primary exercise motive is to enhance one's fitness is also numbers-driven. Individuals with a high need to achieve or have a strong competitive nature (discussed later) will find improving various measures of fitness very appealing. Therefore, it is important that clients receive a series of fitness tests prior to and during their exercise program. Examples include strength, cardiovascular, percent body fat, blood pressure, and flexibility. Chapter 6 discusses these in greater detail. It is equally important that tests are conducted by a qualified fitness instructor (e.g., certified by a national fitness organization), exercise physiologist, or physician.

Improved Psychological and Emotional Health

One of the primary benefits of exercise, particularly relevant for MHPs, is its effectiveness on various types of mental disorders, mood states, and dispositions. Leith (1998) provides extensive support for the ways in which exercise overcomes or at least improves self-concept, depression, stress, anxiety, and overall mental health. He provides plausible explanations of the links between exercise and improved mental health.

Leith (1998) and Anshel, Reeves, and Roth (2003) recommend numerous strategies to address these conditions. These include:

1. pick an exercise that the client finds appealing,

2. avoid feelings of meeting expectations, competitiveness, or any other sources of pressure in an exercise routine,

3. think relaxing thoughts while exercising,

4. listen to the body for stress signals, which is a prompt to exercise,

5. avoid getting carried away with the exercise program (i.e., avoid the "more is better" mentality),

6. be flexible if desired results are not experienced—choose some other form of exercise or redesign the exercise program,

7. exercise to your favorite music,

8. add variety to your workout,

9. obtain social support (e.g., exercise with a friend or family member, obtain personal coaching, participate in group exercise programs), and

10. use proper clothing (e.g., high quality shoes, clothes that allow the skin to evaporate perspiration) and equipment.

Meet Social Needs

For many individuals, the chance to meet and interact with others is a primary exercise motive. My own experience with exercise rehabilitation patients is that the exercise program provides a strong motive for adherence; the patient literally exercises in order to be with others. The MHP could have a role in fostering introductions to others in the fitness venue—for rehabilitation or healthy clients—or at least to ensure that fitness staff is providing opportunities for social support by establishing personal relationships between staff and other participants and among participants.

Manage Stress and Anxiety

While stress and anxiety are not the same condition (see chapter 4 for an explanation), theories abound that help explain the link between exercise and ways to reduce these conditions. Perhaps one of the more popular explanations for this exercise effect is the *distraction hypothesis*. Persons engaging in vigorous physical activity are unlikely to be producing stressful thoughts. In addition, persons will feel less anxiety if they are exercising in a comfortable environment. Their anxiety will increase, however, if they feel self-conscious in a fitness club surrounded by younger, fitter individuals. One implication for using exercise as a stress reducer is to turn off the cell phone and eliminate all work-related and other stressful thoughts. Second, it is imperative to feel comfortable in an exercise environment. Exercising with a friend, especially in the early stages of an exercise program, is particularly important as a form of social support.

Control Weight

Weight control, that is, preventing weight gain or, more commonly, reducing body weight, is among the more popular reasons to exercise. What is less known among many exercisers, however, is that exercise and improved fitness will *not* necessarily be accompanied by weight loss. Exercise tends to *increase*, not decrease, body weight. This is because vigorous physical activity results in two parallel processes; reduced fat and increased muscle tissue. Our body weight is divided into percent body fat and percent lean muscle tissue. Muscle weighs more than fat. Therefore, if exercise produces more muscle while reducing fat, overall body weight will stay the same or *increase*, not decrease. Clients will notice reduced clothes size, but not reduced bodyweight. Thus, sadly, if weight control is a primary exercise motive for the individuals, they will stop exercising if they do not lose weight.

What many individuals do not know is there are many health-related benefits from exercise even for overweight persons. For example, Drs. Steven Blair and Suzanne Brodney (1999) from the Cooper Aerobics Institute in Dallas examined the results of 24 studies that studied links between the effects of aerobic exercise on physiological outcomes and morbidity (disease) and mortality (death) among male adults. The results of these studies indicated that individuals who were overweight or obese received very similar physiological improvements and health-related benefits in response to aerobic and strength training exercises as compared to their normal weight counterparts. The researchers concluded that a person's decision to exercise should not be associated weight loss. This is because exercise itself, even if not accompanied by a loss in weight or body fat, results in very similar physiological benefits as for persons who are not overweight or obese.

The specific conclusions from the Blair and Brodney (1999) study were as follows:

1. "Overweight and obese individuals who are active and fit have lower rates of disease and death than overweight and obese individuals who are inactive and unfit" (p. S659),

2. "Overweight or obese individuals who are active and fit are less likely to develop obesity-related chronic diseases and have early death than normal weight persons who lead sedentary lives" (p. S659), and

3. "Inactivity and low cardiorespiratory fitness are as important predictors of mortality as being overweight or obese" (p. S660).

It was important to restrict the reviewed studies to one gender because there are too many biological factors (e.g., hormones, bone density, body type, normal rates of morbidity and mortality) related to gender that might influence the conclusions of a review of different studies. Clearly, as the authors conclude, a similar review of studies on women only is also warranted.

Competition

Clients with a strong competitive nature will find goal setting, intra-individual comparisons of performance, and record keeping to be important motivators of exercise adherence. However, others will have a preference for inter-individual competitive events, such as racing or power lifting competition as ways to fulfill their competitive needs. A warning is needed to novices whose competitive nature transfers to the fitness area, which might endanger their health. There are many stories of the "Sunday jogger" who is determined to make up for lost time or the under-fit person who enters an endurance running race, both of whom fall victim to a heart attack, sometimes with fatal consequences. Thus, it is imperative that the novice exerciser not become "too competitive" until they have achieved a sufficient fitness level that will allow them to compete in a healthy and fulfilling manner. Poor health and performance failure (i.e., finishing last) are not motivators for long-term exercise adherence. Finally, because competition often requires high intensity exercise, it is also important that their physician give full medical approval to engage in a particular form of physical activity. In my own research, I have detected several clients with hypertension (i.e., high blood pressure) that prevents them from engaging in aerobic testing without their physician's approval.

In summary, MHPs are in a unique position to determine their clients' motives for starting an exercise program, and then to prescribe cognitive (e.g., positive self-talk, psyching up) and behavior strategies (e.g., goal setting, social support, testing) that are compatible with those motives. Providing the right personal, social, and environmental support will markedly foster the client's likelihood of a long-term—hopefully lifelong—commitment to exercise. One way that will help ensure this desirable objective is to build the client's intrinsic motivation.

STRATEGIES FOR IMPROVING INTRINSIC EXERCISE MOTIVATION

To review, intrinsic motivation (IM) is a person's choice to engage in selected behaviors due to feelings of enjoyment, pleasure, competence, and personal fulfillment in the absence of external rewards. The person's behavior is motivated by his or her need to feel competent and self-determining in dealing with their environment. According to Deci (1975), who first developed this theory, "a person's intrinsic need for feelings of competence and self-determination makes him (or her) aware of potential satisfaction, which, in turn, provides the energy for him (or her) to set goals . . . and to behave in such a way as to try to achieve these goals" (p. 100). The importance of building IM toward exercise behavior, therefore, is predicated on strengthening the client's needs that will result in long-term commitment to adhere to an exercise habit.

Review of IM Components and Goals

Before providing sample strategies for building IM in promoting fitness and a lifestyle change toward regular exercise, let's review the components of IM and client goals in reaching IM. First, IM consists of recognizing the person's need to feel *self-determining*, which is a *controlling function*. This means that clients should make the decisions about when and where to begin their exercise program, and the type of exercises that are most appealing. Rarely are activities carried out over the long term when they are imposed on an individual, as opposed to engaging in activities about which the person has made a conscious choice. The second basic component of IM is the need to feel *competent*, an *information function*. Individuals need positive feedback and other supportive messages that provide a sense of *task mastery*. The combined results of these components is the exerciser's *task satisfaction, enjoyment*, the *perception of high ability*, a sense of *achievement and success*, and continued participation.

IM Strategies

Perceived Choice

As indicated earlier, inherent in IM theory is self-determination in which the individual selects exercise goals and types of activities (e.g., resistance training, cardiovascular exercise) needed to reach those goals. While a client's training regimen should include exercises that improve muscular strength, cardiovascular fitness, and flexibility, the most important goal for reaching IM is the client's readiness to engage in each of these types of activities.

"Guarantee" Success

To meet the objective of task mastery and perceived competence, clients should have a sense of accomplishment, receive consistent—but not constant—positive feedback, and information (e.g., fitness test data) that demonstrates improvement.

Social Support

Social support is a high predictor of exercise adherence. It is important that clients not feel they are undertaking this new and challenging journey alone. Praise and other forms of motivational statements, exercise accompaniment and companionship, and instruction are each sources of social support.

Rewards

The use of rewards in promoting IM is controversial among psychology researchers and practitioners. On one hand, a person who engages in a task for the purpose of receiving a reward is reflecting the less desirable extrinsic, not intrinsic, sources of motivation. On the other hand, rewards can enhance IM if the reward is tied to accomplishing a specific task or set of tasks. Thus, receiving a certificate or a t-shirt for perfect fitness class attendance or for finishing—not necessarily winning—a 6-kilometer race is a tangible reward that promotes feelings of competence and success, components of IM. In this way, rewards that are tied to accomplishments and in which the person's motive for participating in an activity is not strictly to receive the reward, but rather, includes fun and enjoyment, will likely raise IM.

Goal Setting

Goals serve the purposes of helping exercisers focus their efforts on desirable tasks which, when performed properly, will lead to desirable outcomes. Setting goals also provides information that reflects accomplishment and success. Goals should be based on specific performance outcomes that are observable or measurable, attainable yet challenging, be stated positively (not negatively), and presented in both short-term and long-term form.

Fun

This is a term rarely used among adults in exercise settings, yet it's central to IM. Activities that are fun—very enjoyable to the individual—are immensely satisfying. Individuals will participate in and adhere to these activities over the long-term. Not taking oneself too seriously, relaxing during the activity, not being judgmental about one's own success and failure, and exercising with friends help make the activity fun.

Taken together, IM is an important aspect of exercise participation. It is typical to avoid activities in which we feel incompetent or do not find enjoyable, while preferring activities in which we are successful and feel a sense of achievement. Given the propensity of unfit individuals to struggle physically and mentally in a new exercise program, it is important to find ways to help novices determine areas of improvement. Proper fitness coaching, teaching mental skills and proper exercise techniques, and obtaining fitness data from testing will promote feelings of enjoyment and success in exercise settings.

Chapter 6

Basic Applied Exercise Physiology for Consultants

It is not the intention of this chapter to require consultants to become exercise physiologists in order to provide appropriate counsel to their clients. However, as a performance counselor who included exercise as a form of behavioral therapy, I found that my understanding of basic exercise physiology allowed me to make valid and important recommendations for beginning an exercise program. In addition, I have found that the vast majority of individuals who begin an exercise program engage in wrong techniques or omit proper procedures that would make the exercise experience more enjoyable and effective. No wonder the rate of dropping out of fitness-related programs is an astronomical 50–60% within the first 3 to 6 months. Therefore, this chapter is included in the book so that MHPs can provide their clients with accurate information that will separate fact from fiction on exercise technique and facilitate a proper approach to starting an exercise program.

IDENTIFYING FITNESS NEEDS

Although each individual's motives for engaging in regular exercise may differ, all of us have very similar fitness needs and must experience similar exercise outcomes. While MHPs are not in the position to prescribe exercise programs, they can determine a client's fitness needs and inform clients how to reach exercise goals. This section addresses what exercise participants need to know before starting and maintaining an exercise program—the principles for becoming physically fit, how to determine the client's individual needs, and finally, providing basic information in getting the client started.

Client Exercise and Fitness Needs

To improve overall fitness, there are three types of exercises in which clients should engage: aerobic, resistance, and flexibility. Aerobic exercise improves cardiovascular fitness by increasing heart rate over a prolonged period of time, preferably between 20 to 30 minutes. How to accomplish this objective will be discussed later in this chapter. *Resistance exercise* improves muscular strength, muscular endurance, and bone density. *Flexibility exercise* is defined as movements that reflect range of motion around a joint or group of joints. If properly performed, flexibility exercises should be conducted at two different times during an exercise routine: (a) after a brief initial aerobic warm-up, lets say, slow jogging or brisk walking for 5 minutes to start off your exercise session; and (b) at the end of the exercise session in which muscles have contracted repeatedly, resulting in tightening and possible stiffness. After the exercise session muscles need to be "stretched out."

Aerobic Exercise

As discussed in chapter 4, aerobic exercise is essential for improved mental health. This is likely due to the infusion of endorphins, a hormone known to create a state of euphoria due to high enjoyment from physical activity. It may also be due to the exerciser's distraction from other, stressful life events and other unpleasant thoughts. Achieving aerobic fitness, however, is very difficult for many individuals. This is because it's very taxing and physically stressful for individuals who lead a sedentary lifestyle. Still, it is essential that clients engage in aerobic fitness because it is directly responsible for most of the health benefits associated with regular exercise. This includes weight control, reduced "bad" cholesterol (low density lipoprotein, or LDL), improved "good" cholesterol (high density lipoprotein, or HDL), lower triglycerides (fat cells in the blood), reduced blood pressure, increased metabolism (the number of calories burned per minute to sustain life), and a stronger cardiac muscle, making the heart more likely to withstand the effects of a heart attack.

Improving cardiovascular fitness requires engaging in aerobic-type exercises, a form of physical activity that elevates the heart rate in order to strengthen the cardiac muscle. To improve cardiovascular fitness clients must move muscles, preferably leg muscles. Because leg muscles are the largest muscles in the body, they require more oxygen during work, which requires raising the heart rate (HR). Here are exercise principles for improving cardiovascular fitness based on the recommendations of the American College of Sports Medicine (ACSM, 2001).

Frequency

To achieve cardiovascular fitness, a person should engage in aerobic exercise from three to five times per week, preferably on alternative days. The body needs time for recovery after vigorous physical activity, so more than five aerobic workouts per week is not recommended so that tissues can heal. The operational term here is *vigorous*, meaning that aerobic exercise is effective if the person is correctly addressing the next principle, intensity.

Intensity

Intensity refers to the heart rate achieved while performing aerobic exercise. Without achieving a *training heart rate* (THR) the heart muscle, like any other muscle in the body, will not become stronger. It must be taxed well beyond resting heart rate (RHR). There are two formulae, both of which are valid and indicate the targeted HR. The easiest for most people to remember is to subtract the person's age from 220 (220 is the predicted maximal HR). Then multiply that score by .6 (60% of predicted maximum HR) for low fit people, or by .7 (70%) or .8 (80%) of predicted maximum, depending on their current fitness level. Thus, an unfit 30-year-old person's THR is: $220 - 30 = 190 \times .6 = 114$ beats per minute (bpm).

A person who is somewhat fit, currently engages in regular aerobic-type exercise, and is not overweight will be able to achieve a higher THR than an unfit, sedentary, overweight individual (220 − 30 × .8 = 161 bpm).

Achieving aerobic fitness is the most challenging of all exercise types because it requires the individual to increase heart rate dramatically, a task not practiced by persons who lead a sedentary lifestyle. Aerobic exercise requires exertion—quite a bit of it—that is something our species was forced to do in order to catch food, run from predators, and survive. The problem is that most individuals do not know how to exercise properly. This leads to a high degree of discomfort, poor results, and too often, eventual withdrawal from physical activity (the exercise dropout).

I observe other exercisers regularly—usually walking—when I run on my campus's indoor track. One of the many common errors committed by novice exercisers is their propensity to under-exert. That is, instead of brisk walking or engaging in "walk-run" intervals, which can increase aerobic fitness, they will "go for a stroll" and hope to increase heart rate at the required level. It cannot happen that way. The issue of proper aerobic exercise techniques will be addressed when describing fundamental prescriptions in this chapter.

Time (Duration)

Another common error I observe among novice exercisers, especially younger exercise participants, is the use of speed rather than duration as the exercise method. The exerciser thinks that the best way to become aerobically fit is to move as quickly as possible. Not surprisingly, the problem becomes burning out due to premature physical fatigue; aerobic fitness is never reached because there is insufficient time to reach and maintain THR. How long, then, should a person engage in aerobic exercise? The answer is from 20 to 30 minutes. This does *not* mean a person is required to exercise for half an hour nonstop to receive the full benefits of aerobic exercise. THR can be reached through interval training, a topic discussed later, which consists of exercising at alternating high and low intensities (e.g., walk-jog intervals).

In summary, then, in order to reach THR and achieve the benefits of cardiovascular exercise, a person should move at an intensity of 60 to 85% of his or her predicted maximum heart rate over a period of 20 to 30 minutes, three to five days a week.

Resistance Training

Muscular strength is defined as the maximal force a muscle or muscle group can generate on one attempt. A test of strength, therefore, is usually determined by the amount of weight a person can lift one time—measured by a one-repetition maximum test.

The principle of strength training is to keep the number of repetitions low, between 6 to 8, and the amount of resistance high, 80–90% of their one-repetition maximum. A general rule of thumb is to have the exerciser lift the amount of resistance that will allow the person to complete 6 to 8 repetitions. If they cannot complete at least 6 repetitions, the weight is too high. If, on the other hand, they can easily go beyond 8 repetitions, the weight is too low.

According to ACSM (2001), muscular fitness is important for overall health because it:

1. Improves bone health;

2. Increases or maintains muscle mass, which increases resting metabolic rate—the number of calories burned to sustain life. This improves weight control.

3. Increases glucose tolerance, which reduces the chance of having type 2 diabetes;

4. Lowers the risk of injury and low back pain;

5. Improves the ability to carry out activities of daily living;

6. Improves balance and decreases risk of falls in older individuals; and

7. Improves self-esteem.

Should strength exercises be performed before or after aerobic work? One school of thought indicates it makes no difference. However, there is a case for performing strength exercises after, not before, aerobic work. Here's why.

1. *The warm-up effect.* Aerobic work increases internal body temperature, which warms up muscles. A warmer muscle contracts with more efficiency and is less susceptible to fatigue.

2. *The fatigue effect.* Aerobic work has already fatigued muscles. It is the goal of resistance training to fatigue the muscle (i.e., the overload principle). Therefore, a muscle already fatigued by aerobic work will be more susceptible to the training effects of resistance training because it is being called upon to perform work beyond this initial fatigue level.

Flexibility Exercise

Improving flexibility will decrease the chance of injury and allow a greater range of motion—more mobility of movement. Stretching is the best way to improve flexibility. Stretching can be performed incorrectly, however. There are two types of stretching techniques, one of which should be avoided.

Static Stretching

This is the correct stretching technique, and is recommended to reduce muscle soreness. It involves slowly stretching a muscle to the point of mild tension and then holding the position for 10–30 seconds.

Ballistic Stretching

This technique involves the use of momentum by repetitive bouncing movements. The problem with ballistic stretching is that your tendons react to the "bouncing"—which is an attempt to maximize the stretch effect—by protecting the muscle. The automated response is to tighten, not loosen, the muscle and the tendon that attaches it to the bone. Therefore, ballistic stretching is counterproductive.

General guidelines for stretching are:

1. Stretch to the point of mild tension or discomfort;

2. Hold each stretch for 10–30 seconds;

3. Keep your back in its natural alignment;

4. Do not lock your joints;

5. Do not hold your breath while stretching;

6. Do not bounce or use momentum;

7. Do not allow the weight-bearing knee to flex more than 90 degrees;

8. Do not hyperextend the neck or lower back.

Six Exercise Principles for Optimal Fitness

The benefits of exercise programs are accrued when individuals follow these six principles. They are valid for experiencing all types of exercise.

Overload Principle

Try picking up a pencil as if you are lifting a dumbbell, flexing at the elbow. Do you think you will actually build up your bicep muscle? Do you think you will increase the strength of your heart—reach training heart rate—by going for a stroll? The answer is "no" in both cases. This is because in order to strengthen muscles—remember, the heart is also a muscle—you have to "overload" it. That means, the muscle must work at a higher level, lift a heavier load or beat at a faster pace than accustomed.

To increase muscular strength or endurance, overload is accomplished by performing the exercise more times than normal, or by adding a greater resistance. To improve the cardiovascular system, overload is accomplished by placing greater than normal demands on the heart and lungs through aerobic activity. Strolling, for example, will not provide sufficient demands on the heart and lungs to warrant a "training effect." The individual needs to walk briskly or engage in alternating high intense–low intense exercise, a technique called interval training (explained later). We must go beyond our comfort zone in order to improve our fitness; we have to overload the system.

Principle of Specificity

This states that the effects of exercise are specific to the muscles involved and the exercises performed. Thus, if a client wants to improve cardiovascular functioning, then they must perform aerobic exercises (e.g., jogging, swimming, biking), because only this form of exercise significantly increases heart rate to improve cardiovascular fitness. If improving muscular strength is the main goal, then lifting weights using the muscles the person desires to strengthen is needed.

Principle of Progression

One of the top reasons people drop out of exercise programs is due to physical discomfort or injury—doing too much too soon. The principle of progression helps prevent this dilemma. The principle states that a person should gradually increase his or her overload over a period of time. The rate of progression is dependent on the person's current fitness level, age, goals, and activity preferences. Exercising too vigorously in the beginning will bring on discomfort, even injury. There are three stages of progression: initial, improvement, and maintenance.

The *initial* stage should include light muscular exercise at low to moderate intensity over a period of 4 weeks, 3 to 4 days per week, each session for 15–20 minutes. Heart rate is 60–70% of maximum. The *improvement* stage typically lasts for 4–5 months, which in time is increased to 20–30 minutes and the intensity is progressively increased to 70–85% of maximum. Finally, the *maintenance* stage usually begins after 5–6 months, but may also start earlier if fitness goals are reached.   .

Principle of Overuse

A companion of the Progression Principle, this principle states that if you do too much too quickly, injuries and other health problems will occur. Overuse usually is represented by an injury to an area that has received too much repetition. Shin splints is a good example of overuse in which the exerciser continues to use a muscle group (the legs) repetitiously until there is a breakdown of tissue; an injury occurs.

Principle of Individuality (or Individual Differences)

Everyone responds to exercise differently, partly due to their genetic predisposition. We are born with different body types, muscle fiber types, and the number of muscle fibers and fat cells. Each of these differences affects the way we respond to exercise, the effects of exercise on our system, and even our exercise preferences. For example, individuals with many muscle fibers—a trait established during gestation—will have a propensity to build larger muscle mass than individuals with relatively fewer muscle fibers. Thus, while each of us is capable of reaching our own capability, we differ on what that capability—our optimal level—is. The answer is to do the best you can when exercising, *and overload!*

Principle of Reversibility (Use and Disuse)

Perhaps you have heard the adage, "If you don't use it, you lose it." Muscles and physiological systems will deteriorate if they are not used regularly. Detraining of some muscle groups and the cardiovascular system will begin within 48 hours of non-use. It is imperative that a person remain active in order to keep fit. Exercising once per week is both ineffective for fitness and dangerous. A person cannot "make up for lost time" when they do not exercise all week, then try to exercise vigorously on Sunday. The individual who tries to overcome a sedentary lifestyle with a once-per-week all-out effort is asking for medical trouble, including a heart attack.

These principles are meant to inform clients that there is a right way to begin and maintain an exercise program to avoid injury and to reach fitness goals. When carrying out an exercise program, each of these principles should be strongly remembered.

FUNDAMENTAL EXERCISE PRESCRIPTIONS

This is an area that is usually reserved for personal trainers and exercise physiologists because providing an exercise prescription should be based on fitness testing data. However, the MHP can play an important role in "getting the ball rolling" by creating a basic exercise program that is safe, nonthreatening, challenging yet achievable, and does not require fitness testing and a fitness club membership. Instead of sending the client off to an uncertain and threatening environment (e.g., the fitness club), and speaking to a stranger (e.g., a personal trainer) about performing very challenging physical tasks, the MHP can serve two important functions: (1) provide the client with emotional support to undertake the task of starting a new exercise program, and (2) generate a sense of optimism and personal control by taking small, initial steps toward achieving fitness and improved mental and physical health. The reason the MHP should master this material is that many clients will be receptive to beginning an exercise program as part of their therapy program. This openness to embarking on a new exercise program to improve health and well-being is partly based on the trust established between MHPs and their clients.

Here are some fundamental components of prescribing an exercise program (also see chapter 7).

I. PHYSICIAN'S APPROVAL

Be sure the client's doctor has performed an examination prior to starting an exercise program. Individuals with high blood pressure, apparent cardiovascular disease, and are overweight or obese are not safe candidates for aerobic exercise. The personal physician will also determine if the client/patient should take a stress test to detect possible heart abnormalities.

II. TESTING

1. *Fitness testing.* The client should receive fitness tests that measure strength, cardiovascular endurance (usually determined with a treadmill walk test or a bicycle submaximal VO^2 test), blood pressure, and percent body fat (to determine what percent of the client's weight is fat versus lean body tissue). Personal trainers or, even better, exercise physiologists or cardiologists should conduct testing of this nature. One valuable purpose of this testing is to provide information about prescribing a proper exercise program based on initial fitness and health level.

2. *Blood testing.* One valuable piece of information that offers great incentive to someone contemplating an exercise program is to have his or her blood tested for cholesterol, referred to as a lipids profile. Cholesterol testing indicates if the individual has too much "bad" cholesterol, not enough "good" cholesterol, and

the extent of fat cells—called triglycerides—in the blood, all of which are predictors of heart disease.

III. INITIAL STEPS

1. *Perceived choice.* One predictor of exercise adherence is what is called *perceived choice*. This means that the client should have a significant role in determining the type of exercises in which to engage—or not engage, at least in the beginning. If they do not want to jog on a running path or prefer to avoid weights, and instead, prefer water aerobics, great. Give them a choice of activities from which to choose to reach their fitness and health goals. On the other hand, we should be suggesting to them what types of exercises are needed to experience their desired benefits. Yoga, for instance, will not improve the cardiovascular system, although it will improve flexibility, promote relaxation, and reduce stress.

What are the client's interests concerning the type(s) of exercise they are prepared to do? Perhaps they have pain or an injury that must be considered before prescribing a program. Someone with a bad back or bad knees or ankles, for example, should not be jogging.

2. *Personal Coaching.* It is highly unlikely your clients will be able to start a program on their own. Determine resources in your community that offer high quality personal coaching, fitness testing, and long-term programs. Fitness clubs (a topic discussed earlier and addressed, again, later) vary greatly in their quality of facilities, service, cleanliness, and sophistication.

3. *Know the basics of improving fitness.* The MHP does not need to be an exercise physiologist to provide fundamental advice for starting an exercise program. Clients should do the following: (a) purchase a good pair of running shoes; (b) start walking briskly, even in their neighborhood, (c) schedule their exercise periods during the week in terms of both days of the week and hour of the day, (d) interval train, in which the exercise moves quickly (i.e., a "work" interval consisting of brisk walking, even light jogging for 2–3 minutes) following by intervals of less intense

movement (i.e., the "rest" interval consisting of walking if the person was jogging during their work interval, or slower walking if the person was walking very briskly).

4. *Use the Exercise Checklist located in Appendix A.* This list provides guidelines for proper exercise preparation and action. For example, clients should drink water all during the day, but especially within 15 minutes of their exercise and at regular intervals during their exercise session. After the session they should pay special attention to hydration needs. Drink up. It is likely that we are dehydrated due to our propensity to avoid sufficient water intake during the day.

5. *Avoid overstraining.* Exercise at least three times a week, spread out over the week. Do not "make up for lost time" by exercising too long or hard in one session.

6. *Suggest sources of social support.* Your client will need the spiritual and, perhaps, physical support of friends, family, and professionals. Clearly, exercise adherence is far better if novice exercisers have someone from whom they are receiving emotional support (e.g., "I'm proud of you for starting to exercise"), or someone with whom to exercise, a form of physical support. It is helpful if an exercise facility offers clients a personal trainer who can teach the novice how to start a program, use the equipment properly, and become comfortable attending the facility.

7. *Follow the general principles of fitness.* There are a set of general guidelines for starting an exercise program, and MHPs should be able to follow these in prescribing exercise for their clients. They are (in addition to finding a personal trainer):

(a) Have realistic goals; it did not take 2 weeks to get into your current physical condition, and it will not take 2 weeks to become fit and healthier. There will be discomfort because when we exercise and raise the heart rate or increase muscular strength, we are placing stress on our system for which it is unaccustomed. This is why the process of exercise over time to improve fitness is called "training."

(b) Ritualize your fitness session; schedule it, find a friend with whom to exercise, and maintain that schedule.

(c) The key to improving fitness and health is increasing your heart rate to—or near—training level. You can't take a stroll and think you will experience the health benefits of aerobic exercise. You must move quickly and increase your heart rate substantially.

(d) Warm up properly. This means start walking before jogging. Or, if you choose bicycling or swimming, engage in some low-key activity before moving more intensely. Warm-up allows your system to slowly increase the flow of blood and oxygen to the working muscles.

(e) Think INTERVAL TRAINING. It is not recommended that you start running nonstop, and then consider your workout complete when you fatigue. Instead, improve aerobic capacity by engaging in work-rest intervals. For example, you might perform repeated bouts of 3 minutes of brisk walking followed by 1 minute of slower walking, or, if you are more fit, 3 minutes of jogging followed by 1 minute of walking for a period of 20 to 30 minutes, depending on your fitness level.

(f) *Stretching.* One of the great exercise *myths* is that you need to stretch before you exercise more vigorously. Not true, and several studies have shown that there is no advantage to stretching before a regular exercise session. You *should* stretch, however, *after* your aerobic workout because muscles have been contracting repeatedly, and they tend to remain partially contracted after a prolonged exercise bout. They need to be stretched, using the static stretching technique (i.e., holding the stretched position for 3 seconds).

(g) *Hydration.* Be sure you drink plenty of water before, during (that's right, take a quick break and drink during your exercise), and immediately after your workout.

(h) *Resistance training.* It is important to include resistance training in your exercise routine. Either purchase weights for your home or use the weight room at your local fitness club. Do not neglect this aspect of fitness; it will improve bone strength, reduce the chance of injury, and increase your metabolism at rest (i.e., the number of calories you burn while sedentary to sustain life). A higher metabolism will result in improved weight control.

COMMON ERRORS OF BEGINNING EXERCISERS

There is a science to proper exercise. I attend my university's exercise center and observe hundreds of people making important mistakes in their exercise preparation and performance. The tragedy of making mistakes before and during exercise is that exercise outcomes will be poorer than if exercise was executed properly. Desired results are not achieved. Try to avoid the following.

1. *Lack of hydration.* Many of us are probably dehydrated (do not have sufficient water in our system) about 80% of the time (Groppel, 2000). Water is life-sustaining; we need it more than we think. Water rids the body of natural toxins that build up from normal bodily functions, including ridding the system of bacteria. The failure to drink sufficient amounts of water not only leads to dehydration, but also contributes to fatigue, illness, and eventually, kidney failure. We need at least 64 ounces of water daily, much more than most of us drink. Water fountains are helpful, but we tend to drink too little water from a fountain as opposed to bottles and cups. We feel the "wet and cold" sensations by just a few sips of water, but the actual amount of water we take in is not enough. We need to gulp, not sip it. Exercise exacerbates the need for water due to sweating. Drink up.

2. *Pre-exercise stretching.* What a waste of time. I am convinced most people who stretch before exercising are actually procrastinating from starting the "hard part," beginning their aerobic workout. Pre-exercise stretching is simply a myth; there are no benefits unless you are an elite athlete who makes very rapid movements at varying angles that require extensive joint flexibility. Once you are ready to start your exercise session, pass on the stretching. Instead, stretch *after* your exercise session, not before it.

3. *Thinking speed, not endurance.* Younger exercisers—who I see on my campus's jogging track all the time—think sprinting around the track is the primary goal of their workout. Not surprisingly, they tire easily and then leave the track after a mere 3 to 5 minutes of exercise, not even sufficient to have an aerobic benefit. Slow down—remember interval training—and prolong the exercise bout.

4. *Insufficient duration.* The research is clear on this: we need to engage in aerobic exercise from 20 to 30 minutes. Too many of us think we have ended our aerobic workout when we are fatigued, break a sweat, or run out of energy. Perhaps we are finished when we reach an end point, let's say three laps around the track or from "here" to "there." Instead, exercise should consume more time than we think; distance should not be the main criterion of our "finish line." Think "minutes."

5. *Wrongly thinking distance, not time.* Similar to the previous point, we need to stop thinking of *distance* as the main exercise goal, and instead, think of *time.* I jog on my university's indoor track for 30 minutes (using interval training), which includes a 2-minute warm-up consisting of brisk walking. My watch is affixed to my left wrist to remind me of the time I have remaining, a motivational tool that also allows me to monitor my exercise time.

6. *Continuous, not interval, training.* One reason we quit exercising prematurely is that we think we have to exercise nonstop (continuously) until we get tired or reach some predetermined goal. However, we do not reach *training heart rate.* Our heart rate during continuous training reaches optimum well below the training level. The only way to have a "training effect" on our cardiovascular system (in which the heart muscle is strengthened) is to interval train (discussed earlier). Exercising on work and rest intervals raises the heart rate to sufficient intensity that allows a training effect.

Given these myths about exercise and our propensity to do the wrong thing, why do we continue to exercise incorrectly? The answer is simple; no one is teaching us to exercise properly. Our physical education majors who are not taught proper exercise techniques, do not learn to lead exercise classes, and often do not complete a single course in fitness management or applied exercise physiology. Along these lines, university professors do not teach our students these techniques. The only avenue to acquire this information is by being certified as a fitness instructor, which excludes 99.9% of the population. This is our dilemma; we are a country of exercisers who are uninformed about the proper ways to exercise. This book is an attempt to help remedy this problem, or at least to provide one profession, MHPs, with the knowledge to help others in this area.

CONCLUDING COMMENTS

This chapter is not intended to train MHPs to prescribe proper exercise programs. Instead, it was meant to provide fundamental knowledge about proper preparation for engaging in an exercise routine that will create optimal outcomes and meet client needs. The MHPs' goals are to help clients have the courage and confidence to begin and maintain a regular exercise habit. By all means, MHPs should refer their clients to professionals who are licensed personal trainers and accredited by the American College of Sports Medicine (ACSM), or to a university professor in exercise physiology who could provide proper exercise testing and prescription. However, because of the trust that MHPs engender in their clients, this profession provides a very important opportunity to make a vast impact on the mental health of their clients through exercise. MHPs need to go beyond the vague suggestion to their clients, "try exercising." Instead, clients need to feel more secure about undertaking this very challenging and threatening task; they need more details and direction.

Chapter 7

Exercise Prescription Strategies

Exercise prescription is "the process of designing a regimen of physical activity in a systematic and individualized manner" (ACSM, 2001, p. 230). The primary objective of exercise prescription is to facilitate positive changes in a client's personal physical activity program. Why would a MHP be concerned about this information? Should a MHP be trained to conduct fitness tests and prescriptions? Would it not be more appropriate for a fitness leader, personal trainer, or exercise physiologist to provide exercise prescriptions rather than individuals who are not trained in this area? Yes, to all of these questions. However: (a) not all so-called "specialists" are trained to prescribe exercise programs, (b) when an exercise program is prescribed, it is often without the benefit of fitness test data from which to make accurate exercise suggestions, (c) some MHPs are in a unique position to make at least fundamental, or approximate, exercise prescriptions because they have gained the trust of their client, who otherwise may not take the initiative to be tested or receive an exercise prescription from a personal trainer, and (d) it is important for MHPs to know this area so that he or she can make judgments about the appropriateness of the prescription their clients have received. Thus, this chapter will consist of reviewing fitness prescription techniques that reflect proper basic principles of improving fitness.

FITNESS PRESCRIPTION GUIDELINES

The Centers for Disease Control and Prevention and ACSM recommend adults perform exercises consisting of five components: (1) frequency, (2) duration, (3) intensity, (4) mode, and (5) progression.

- Aerobic activity should be performed 30 or more minutes of exercise each day at moderate intensity.

- Aerobic activity should be performed either in a single session or accumulated throughout the day in multiple bouts, lasting 8–10 minutes per bout.

- The *minimum* training intensity threshold is 40–50% of heart rate reserve (i.e., a percentage of the person's predicted maximal heart rate), although exercise psychologists recommend 60 to 85% to receive the benefits of aerobic exercise.

- Previously inactive men over age 40, women over age 50, and people at high risk for cardiovascular disease should first consult a physician before embarking on a program of vigorous physical activity to which they are unaccustomed.

- Strength-developing activities (resistance training) should be conducted at least twice per week. A minimum of 8–10 strength-developing exercises that use the major muscle groups (legs, trunk, arms, and shoulders) should be performed at each session. One or two sets of 8–12 repetitions of each exercise is recommended.

The Physical Activity Pyramid

Nieman (2003) describes a model developed by ACSM that combines lifestyle and formal approaches to exercise prescriptions based on the exerciser's individual needs.

The Lifestyle Approach

Located at the base of the pyramid, this approach reflects the need for all healthy individuals to accumulate at least 30 minutes of physical activity nearly every day. The lifestyle approach is for the general public to recognize the importance of daily, preferably vigorous, physical activity.

Formal Approach

The formal exercise program is located at stages 2 and 3 of the activity pyramid. Increased aerobic fitness occurs by brisk walking, swimming, cycling, running, or engaging in active sports for 20–60 minutes, 3–5 days per week. The formal approach also includes improving muscular fitness by lifting weights, engaging in hard physical labor, and stretching. A minimum of 8–10 separate exercises that train major muscle groups should be performed. Performers should complete one set of 8–12 repetitions of each exercise to the point of fatigue at least 2–3 days per week. To enhance flexibility, stretching should occur 2–3 days per week and consist of four repetitions of several stretches that are held 10–30 seconds at a position of mild discomfort (a technique called static stretching). Finally, it is recommended that sitting time (e.g., watching TV, computer work, playing videos) should be significantly reduced.

FITNESS PRESCRIPTION TECHNIQUES

This section will take us through the four primary components of an exercise session: warm-up, stretching, aerobic activity, and cooldown. A separate section will be devoted to exercises that improve muscular tone that address specific muscle groups (e.g., sit-ups, push-ups, leg raises).

Warm-up

Warm-up is defined as a group of exercises performed immediately before an activity, which provides the body with a period of adjustment from rest to exercise" (Neiman, 2003, p. 236). The purposes of warming up are to increase internal body temperature, increase the flow of red blood cells (i.e., oxygen) to working muscles, which reduces fatigue, and improve the speed of nerve impulses. Warm-up reduces risk of injury and prepares the body for more vigorous physical activity. A warm-up should take between 5–15 minutes, depending on the task and the environmental temperature (Anshel et al., 2003).

One particular myth concerning warming up is the need to stretch as the first task. This is a waste of time unless you are nursing a muscle injury or plan on competing in elite sport in which muscles will be contracted at excessive speeds. Instead, exercisers should jog lightly and slowly prepare the body for more vigorous activity. It is now believed that flexibility exercises be performed *after* mild warm-up activity for 5–10 minutes. Stretching will then be safer and more productive.

The type of stretching also is important for enhancing flexibility. As indicated earlier, there are two stretching styles, *ballistic* and *static*. *Ballistic stretching* "involves the use of momentum by repetitive bouncing movements to stretch a muscle. This type of stretch can produce muscle soreness or injury if the movement is too great" (Anshel et al., 2003). It is best to avoid ballistic stretching at all times. It is a myth that "bouncing" produces a better stretch. In fact, just the opposite is true. The "bouncing" motion causes a reflex in the tendons to *prevent*, not facilitate, stretching the affected muscle. Tendons attach a muscle to the bone. The reflex prevents the muscle from tearing, and the tendon from tearing away from the bone. It's a defensive mechanism. *Static stretching*, by far the safest and most effective style, consists of holding a position to the point of mild tension, then maintaining the stretched position from 10 to 30 seconds.

Here are some guidelines for proper stretching.

- Stretch to a point of mild tension or discomfort;

- Hold each stretch for 10–30 seconds;

- Keep your back straight in its natural alignment;

- Do not lock your joints;

- Do not hold your breath while performing a stretch, maintain regular breathing;

- Do not bounce or use momentum;

- Never allow a weight bearing knee to flex more than 90 degrees;

- Do not hyperextend the neck or lower back; and

- With each standing stretch, keep abdominals tight, back straight, and knees slightly bent.

Finally, there are proper and improper ways to stretch, a topic that goes beyond the scope of this chapter. Several books are on the market that explain and illustrate proper stretching technique.

CARDIOVASCULAR (AEROBIC) EXERCISE

There are three principles to remember when prescribing cardiovascular exercise, frequency (how often per week), intensity (how high heart rate should go), and duration (the number of minutes in an exercise session). It is in this area, frequency, intensity, and duration, where most people underachieve and fail to experience the full benefits of exercise.

Frequency

A minimum of three days per week with no more than two days between workouts is recommended to achieve aerobic fitness. Even the days in which exercise is intense can be offset with "off days" in which exercise is still performed, but at lower intensity (e.g., brisk walking, weights, recreational pursuits in which it is not necessary to monitor heart rate). However, on "aerobic days," clients should attempt to reach a target heart rate (discussed in the next section, and in chapter 6).

Intensity

Intensity level refers to heart rate that must be achieved to obtain a cardiovascular benefit. It is usually the most challenging requirement to meet because it is uncomfortable due to our sedentary lifestyle. Help your clients determine their training heart rate (THR), the rate at which a training effect is reached. The heart is a muscle and, like any muscle, improves its efficiency and strength when sufficient demands are placed upon it. This concept is not unlike lifting a weight at sufficient resistance that causes the muscle to enlarge because it adapts to the increased weight—actually, the muscle fibers split; when the muscle fiber repairs itself through protein synthesis it develops a wider radius, hence a larger muscle. Thus, a person's heart rate must be sufficient to improve efficiency. Exercisers cannot go for a stroll and experience a training effect. Instead, we want clients to attempt to reach their THR.

The technique for reaching THR is not sprinting, then fatiguing. And it does not consist of continuous training in which the exerciser moves nonstop at a consistent rate of speed. Instead, the technique is called *interval training (IT)*. IT consists of exercising at varying speeds, or intervals. An interval could be a series of 3–5 minutes of high intensity exercise, let's say, running or rapid bicycling, followed by a period of reduced exercise intensity, let's say 1–2 minutes of brisk walking or reduced bicycling speed. In summary, IT could include 5 minutes high intensity movement followed by 2 minutes of less intense exercise, a cycle repeated 5 times to equal a proper duration that ensures all benefits will be accrued (discussed in the next section).

Duration

When I run on my university's indoor track, I observe (mostly male) students running for speed rather than for endurance. They tend to go about 2–3 laps, burn out, then depart thinking they had a good workout. Sadly, they missed the primary health benefits of exercise. It is not speed, but duration, that counts most in aerobic exercise. The person burns more calories, reduces "bad" (LDL) cholesterol and triglycerides (blood fat), and improves mood state if engaging in sufficient duration—not speed.

What is the length of time a person should exercise aerobically that will provide optimal health and fitness benefits? Nieman (2003) suggests "beginners should start with 10–20 minutes of aerobic activity, those in average shape should go for 20–30 minutes of aerobic activity, and highly fit people can exercise for 30–60 minutes" (p. 247). For health benefits, the ACSM recommends exercising for *at least* 30 minutes at a moderate-intensity level during the day. This means that exercise benefits are the same whether the person splits up exercise periods during the day or completes activity all at once.

Taking intensity and duration into account to improve aerobic fitness, it is recommended that the person should: (1) perform at

40–60% of maximal heart rate or higher, several times a week (this will burn 200–400 calories per day), and (2) engage in aerobic exercise 4–5 days per week with each session lasting 20–30 minutes.

TYPES OF EXERCISE

Various forms of exercise serve different needs. The main types of exercises that will meet the fitness and health needs of most individuals include resistance training, cardiovascular—also called aerobic—training, and flexibility.

Resistance Training

The purpose of resistance training, also called strength training, is to increase muscular strength, muscular endurance, and muscle size. The reason resistance training increases the size of muscle mass is because using a certain muscle group to lift a weight results in tearing many muscle fibers. The fibers "adapt" to these new demands in the repair process by increasing its diameter. A larger muscle results. This is why a person's muscular size is dependent on the number of fibers he or she has (which is genetically determined). Hence, not every male can appear like "Mr. Universe" and also explains why most females can't develop a musculature similar to a male; optimal muscle size is genetically limited by the number of muscle fibers with which we were born.

According to ACSM (2001) guidelines for resistance training in healthy adults, the primary goal is to engage in a program that allows developing total body strength in a "reasonable" period of time. Programs longer than one hour per session are associated with higher dropout rates. The following prescription is recommended:

1. Perform a minimum of 8–10 separate exercises that train the major muscle groups.

2. Perform one set of 8–12 repetitions of each of these exercises to the point of volitional fatigue. For persons older then the age of 50 years, 10–15 repetitions may be more appropriate.

3. These exercises should be performed at least 2–3 days per week. ACSM indicates that, while more frequent training and

additional sets or combinations of sets and repetitions elicit larger strength gains, the additional improvement is relatively small.

4. Effective resistance training is dependent on correct techniques for performing each exercise.

5. Perform every exercise with a full range of motion.

6. Perform both the lifting and lowering portion of the resistance exercises in a controlled manner.

7. Maintain a normal breathing pattern; holding one's breath can induce excessive increases in blood pressure.

8. If possible, exercise with a training partner who can provide feedback on technique, assistance on selected exercises, and be a source of motivation (social support).

A weight-training program requires knowledge of certain concepts.

Repetitions to Fatigue

Repetitions below 3–5 resulting in muscular fatigue produces optimal muscular strength. Repetitions greater than 15–25 improves muscular endurance.

Sets

One set (which consists of a selected number of repetitions) is appropriate for beginners, however, 3–5 sets are needed for gains in optimal strength and muscle size.

Rest Between Sets

Advanced weight lifters have a shorter rest interval—about 1–2 minutes. Novices should rest 2–3 minutes between sets.

Order of Exercise

Some lifters exercise the large muscle groups first, while others start out with small muscle groups. Order of exercise does not seem to matter.

Cardiovascular Training

Cardiovascular training usually consists of brisk walking, running/ jogging, hiking, swimming, skating, bicycling, rowing, cross-country skiing, rope skipping, and various endurance sports. One form of activity that has gained increasing popularity in recent years is brisk walking (see chapter 6).

Brisk Walking

Walking for exercise is one of the fastest growing forms of exercise in the U.S. From the perspective of public health and a growing problem with weight control, brisk walking is probably the best overall exercise for the majority of American adults (Nieman, 2003). According to Nieman, "walking has a higher compliance rate than other physical activities because it can easily be incorporated into a busy time schedule, does not require any special skills, equipment, or facility, is companionable, and is much less apt to cause injuries" (p. 248). Brisk walking can be used to improve aerobic capacity.

What are the criteria for an effective walking program? To use scientific criteria, researchers have found that "a walking pace equal to 60% VO^2 max has been found to increase the VO^2 max of previously sedentary adults 10–20% within 5–20 weeks" (Nieman, 2003, p. 248). The use of visual feedback from heart rate monitors often improves the chances of reaching and maintaining appropriate training heart rates.

Exercise Schedules: Interval vs. Continuous Training

Too often I see joggers, often unfit, run nonstop until they fatigue—perhaps after only a few minutes—and then leave the jogging area and perform calisthenics. These individuals have not experienced the full benefits of cardiovascular exercise such as strengthening the heart muscle by reaching one's target (training) heart rate, burning more calories per minute than any other form of exercise, improving mood state, and an array of other benefits. These joggers are practicing continuous training. While this is effective for more advanced runners, a more effective approach to aerobic training consists of interval training (IT).

IT consists of a series of relatively brief exercise periods usually performed at a high level of intensity, alternating with shorter, less intense periods (Anshel et al., 2003). Examples would include alternating periods of running and walking, or running at high speed alternating with lower jogging periods. The intervals are repeated for a period of 15–30 minutes, depending on the person's fitness level. The main advantage of IT is that it allows the exerciser to reach a training heart rate over a longer period of time. This is because each running bout increases heart rate more with each successive bout. The rest interval decreases heart rate as compared to the work bout, but the heart rate remains slightly higher with each rest period. Therefore, heart rate climbs slowly closer to training level with each work-rest interval. This has been called "the staircase phenomenon" (Anshel & Reeves, 1998) because increased heart rate over time resembles a staircase (see Figure 7.1).

Continuous training, on the other hand, consists of running nonstop over the desired period of time without any rest periods. Heart rate, however, reaches what is called a *steady state*, meaning it is consistent and tends not to reach training level. The primary advantage of continuous training is that less intense exercise burns fat as a primary fuel source, whereas high intensity IT exercise burns carbohydrates. This is one reason distance runners tend to eat

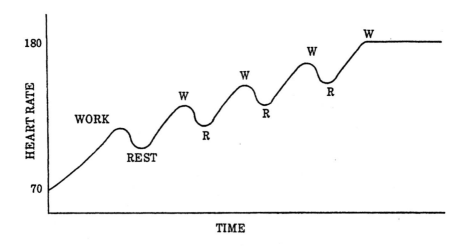

FIGURE 7.1   Increased heart rate during interval training.

considerable amounts of carbohydrates in the days leading up to their race. In summary, if weight loss is a primary goal of aerobic work, the continuous training at lower intensity is often preferred. However, marked improvement in cardiovascular fitness is obtained by reaching training heart rate, obtained primarily through IT. Finally, the beginning exerciser will benefit more from IT than continuous aerobic exercise if their exercise intensity is low to moderate. In other words, the novice exerciser will fatigue prematurely if exercising at high intensity. Instead, the novice's work bout should be relatively brief—let's say about 1–3 minutes, followed by less intense exercise for half the time of their work bout (e.g., a 4:2 or 2:1 work-rest ratio). The result will be exercising longer and at higher intensity.

Flexibility Training

According to ACSM (2001), flexibility is characterized by a person's capability to adapt to new and changing requirements in range of motion occurring at one or more joints. Increased flexibility improves fluidity, ease, coordination, and responsiveness of movement, and reduces the frequency of joint-related injury.

Benefits of Increased Flexibility

While some individuals spend far more time stretching than necessary for good health and exercise preparation, certainly improved flexibility has several advantages. These include:

- Reduced muscle tension and increased relaxation,
- Ease of movement,
- Improved coordination through greater ease of movement,
- Increased range of motion,
- Injury prevention,
- Improvement and development of body awareness,
- Improved circulation and air exchange,
- Decreased muscle viscosity (thickness), causing contractions to be easier and smoother, and
- Decreased soreness associated with other exercise.

Precautions for Flexibility Training

ACSM recommends ways to conduct flexibility training properly to obtain its benefits. These include:

- Stretch a joint through limits of normal *range of motion* (ROM) only.

- Avoid stretching at healed fracture sites for 8–12 weeks postfracture.

- For clients with osteoporosis, stretch with particular caution.

- Avoid aggressive stretching of tissues that have been immobilized (e.g., cast or splinted). Tissues become dehydrated and lose strength during immobilization.

- Recovery time from mild soreness should be no longer than 24 hours. A longer recovery time means the stretching force was excessive.

- Physical performance can vary from day to day for various psycho-biological reasons.

- Set individual goals *unless* goal setting creates tension and is undesirable.

Who Should and Should Not Stretch?

Almost everyone benefits from stretching, individuals of all fitness levels, children as much as adults, and males and females. Pregnant women should not stretch, however, because is can lead to a condition called *hypermobility* of the low back, and other areas. This is because during pregnancy a hormone called *relaxant* softens the ligaments and connective tissue, especially in the pelvic region. Stretching is also not recommended for the relatively few individuals who have naturally loose ligaments and connective tissue. Because joint stability should always be maintained, full range-of-motion stretching may be excessive for these hypermobile individuals.

When to Stretch

This is an area of some controversy due to conflicting scientific evidence. It is thought that stretching before engaging in aerobic exercise or resistance training is unnecessary and less effective than stretching *after* one's regular workout. Several studies have shown that warm-up with light activity before stretching is recommended because warm muscle tissue accepts stretch easier than cold (ASCM, 2001; Anshel et al., 2003). Stretching is particularly beneficial under two conditions: (a) after an exercise session in which muscles have been contracting repeatedly in a rapid manner and, as a result, the muscle remains partially contracted, and (b) after being immobile for long periods of time, especially during or after a long drive.

HOME EXERCISE EQUIPMENT

The use of exercise equipment for home use has gained more popularity then ever before as so many individuals attempt to battle conditions of overweight and obesity in a private setting. Public exercise facilities and programs cause discomfort and anxiety for many individuals. Sadly, exercise equipment purchased for home use often goes unused after a relatively short time. There are no strict guidelines for purchasing home exercise equipment; the decision to exercise at home versus a public facility usually depends on many personal factors. For example, one's comfort level exercising in a public setting, financial resources and space to purchase and store home equipment, financial resources to obtain and retain a fitness club membership, motivational issues related to exercising with others rather than alone, and the need for social support are all criteria for determining the exercise venue.

Nieman (2003) and Jung and Nieman (2000) make the following recommendations for purchasing home exercise equipment.

1. *Determine your personal goals.* Equipment should be selected based on goals for improving strength, flexibility, or cardiovascular fitness. It is important to remember that a single piece of equipment will not likely improve all three areas.

2. *Test equipment prior to purchasing.* Try out the equipment you want to purchase by visiting a fitness equipment store or an exercise facility.

3. *Be cautious of overly optimistic claims.* Remember those extreme, preposterous claims on television about losing fat and

building muscle, sometimes while relaxing? Advertisements of equipment "promising" extraordinary (desirable) changes in body weight, fat, and muscle, none of which are based on scientific evidence, are not new. The consumer, however, must beware of these claims. As Nieman correctly contends, "a workout that is 'easy' or 'effortless' is not likely to provide any true benefit" (p. 251). For example, it is not possible to reduce fat in a specified area of your body, often called *spot reducing.*

4.   *Be cautious of "scientific evidence."* Studies cannot be conducted on every segment of the population. Therefore, it is possible that the results of some studies are based on a very narrow sample and cannot be generalized to your client, or the average person. Was the study reputable? Was it financially supported by the equipment company and carried out in a scholarly manner? Was the study published in a refereed scientific journal? Is a professional organization endorsing the product and the research findings?

5.   *Read the fine print.* An advertiser might contend that results are only possible when combined with a proper diet or supplemental exercise.

6.   *General knowledge.* Nieman contends that "exercising at a specific heart rate will burn a similar number of calories regardless of the piece of equipment used (assuming duration is similar). Claims that one piece of equipment burns more calories than another is likely due to incorporation of larger muscle groups, resulting in an increase heart rate" (p. 251).

7.   *Be an informed consumer.* The quality of exercise equipment and the claims of manufacturers can be verified through information provided by the Federal Trade Commission's Consumer Response Center (www.ftc.gov) or the American Council on Exercise (ACE) (www.acefitness.org).

RECOMMENDED HOME-BASED EXERCISE PROGRAM

Given the above information, what type of exercise program should the MHP recommend to clients who wish to exercise at home? After addressing the client's goals, exercise preferences, willingness to purchase equipment, and clearance from the client's physician to engage in regular exercise, ACSM recommends brisk walking and indoor stationary bicycling, supported with calisthenics for general muscle toning.

The First Month

Each workout should consist of three segments: a warm-up, exercise, and warm down. During the first month, the client should warm up with range-of-motion calisthenics and walk for 5–10 minutes, followed by 15 minutes of brisk walking or stationary cycling at 50–60% of their predicted maximal heart rate ($220 -$ age $\times .5$ or $.6$) 3 days per week. After warming down, the client should engage in static stretching activities—holding the stretched position for 15—20 seconds and do this for 5–10 minutes, followed by toning calisthenics for 10–15 minutes. *Stretching prior to exercise is unnecessary.* Stretching after exercise would be of greater benefit to muscles, which have been repeatedly contracting.

After the First Month

After the first month has past, the duration of brisk walking or cycling should be increased gradually to 30–45 minutes per session, 5–6 days per week. Exercise intensity, the primary criterion for fitness level, can be gradually increased to 70% of predicted maximal heart rate (up to 85% after 90 days of an aerobic training program). Combined with proper dietary habits, these increases in exercise intensity will markedly contribute to steady weight loss, improved physical fitness—typically about one pound per week. Clients should expect marked improvements in blood pressure, cholesterol and other blood test results, improved physical appearance, more positive mood state, more energy during the day, and higher quality of life.

To help ensure sustained motivation, attainment of goals, and long-term exercise adherence, it is recommended that clients be tested every 3 months. Other factors related to long-term adherence include positive support from family and friends, exercising with a companion (if exercise is conducted outside the home), setting reasonable yet challenging goals, establishing rewards for attaining goals (unrelated to food consumption, such as purchasing new clothes or taking a vacation), and combating time obstacles by scheduling exercise sessions on specific days and times. Over time, these scheduled exercise sessions will become ritualized as a normal part of the client's week.

EXERCISE PRESCRIPTION STRATEGIES

Nieman (2003) suggests the following ways to promote long-term compliance to an exercise program.

- Encourage group participation or exercising with a partner.
- Emphasize variety and enjoyment in the exercise program.
- Minimize musculoskeletal injuries with a moderate exercise intensity and a slow rate of progression.
- Help the client determine reasonable goals and highlight these in a contract the client signs.
- Recruit the client's spouse or significant other for support.
- Provide progress charts to document achievement of goals.
- Recognize accomplishments through a system of rewards.
- Maximize convenience concerning time, travel, and family disruptions.
- Complement fitness activities with nutrition education, stress management, and other health-promoting activities to improve the client's overall health and quality of life.

Chapter 8

Exercise Adherence and Compliance

Beginning an exercise habit is challenging, but maintaining it is even more difficult. Sadly, approximately 50% of exercise participants discontinue exercising in structured programs within the first 6 months of starting, although researchers are uncertain if any of these individuals exercise on their own. Chapter 2 reviewed the reasons people start and then drop out of exercise programs. These reasons are collectively called *exercise barriers*. There are many of them, and the result has been a catastrophic effect on the collective health and quality of life of millions of people. Earlier in this book we addressed the array of strategies available to help clients start an exercise program. This chapter addresses what MHPs can do to help clients adhere to it.

DEFINING TERMS

The tendency of a person to maintain participation in an exercise program, or any behavioral regimen, for that matter, once the individual has agreed to undertake it is called *adherence*. In the medical literature, Rand and Weeks (1998) broadly define adherence as "the degree to which patient behaviors coincide with the clinical recommendations of health care providers" (p. 115). Other definitions of adherence include: (a) sticking, or faithfully conforming, to a standard of behavior in order to meet some goal, and (b) long-term behavior changes associated with preventing undesirable symptoms or outcomes. One concept that is often used interchangeably with adherence, but is not the same thing, is called *compliance.*

Compliance refers to behaviors related to following immediate or short-term advice, a direct prescription to improve health or well being, or a sense of coercive obedience to in response to an order. In calling for more compliance research in the health care industry, Nancy Miller and her colleagues (1997) define compliance as "the extent to which recommendations are followed and defined" (p. 1085). Thus, persons who initiate and maintain an exercise program *on one's own volition* are adhering rather than complying with their program. However, persons who are given instructions about what exercise to do and how to do it and carry out these instructions are *complying* with the exercise program. If they permanently stop exercising, again, on their own free will, they are not adhering, and if they do not fulfill the wishes of an authority figure to carry out an exercise regimen (let's say, their personal trainer or a cardiologist who prescribed postcoronary exercise for rehabilitation purposes) they are noncompliers. Despite differences in how adherence and compliance are operationally defined, most authors in this literature continue to use the terms interchangeably.

ADHERENCE ISSUES

Rand and Weeks (1998) address a common problem in the adherence literature—the lack of specific criteria to provide the "gold standard" for determining adherence. What is acceptable adherence in one study or for one exerciser might be non-adherence in another study or for someone else. As indicated earlier, adherence may be classified as "appropriate," "involuntary," "erratic/partial," "ideal," or "voluntary." While a complete review of this area goes beyond the purpose of this section, three points are worth noting from an applied perspective in working with exercise clients. First, labeling someone as an exercise dropout (i.e., a non-adherer) has consequences for long-term intrinsic motivation to persist at future attempts at exercising. The person will conclude, "I once tried that and quit." They will less likely feel secure and motivated to try again. Instead, it might be more motivating to point out limitations in their current exercise habit (i.e., erratic, or partial, adherence) and to build on their strengths (e.g., "You are off to a good start; keep trying because exercise gets easier as you get fitter").

Second, while exercise adherence is usually determined by the extent to which the person is maintaining the original exercise plan, there are often fair reasons for not continuing. One example is the lack of proper instruction, leading to poor exercise technique, higher perceived exertion (i.e., feelings associated with exercise intensity and effort), and greater difficulty in completing the planned routine. Other reasons include sustaining an injury, self-consciousness about one's appearance in an exercise facility, engaging in an exercise activity that one finds overly strenuous, failure to quickly meet goals (which may be unrealistic), and the lack of social support. Researchers have also determined that the absence of an exercise facility located near home or work, job-related travel, physical and mental fatigue, lack of interest, poor weather, family demands, and perceived lack of time, may all lead to discontinuing an exercise plan.

The third point worth noting is the tendency of researchers to collect and publish their data based on formal group exercise programs, as opposed to a person's preference to exercise alone, perhaps at home. In other words, while individuals might decide against continuing to exercise in a structured setting, they could continue to engage in a program of vigorous physical activity on their own. This does not mean they have dropped out, but rather, they have selected another type of venue and structure within which to exercise. To refer to this person as nonadhering to exercise would be incorrect. More research is needed on exercise habits and adherence rates outside of formal exercise program settings.

In her review of the intervention literature, Ockene (2001) notes three levels of factors that affect adherence, the individual, the interpersonal, and the environment. I will link Ockene's concepts to exercise settings.

The Individual

Each individual brings a vast array of previous experiences, personal characteristics (i.e., demographics), knowledge, attitudes, emotions, outcome expectations, and skills to any given situation. Individuals are more likely to exercise if: (a) they understand the benefits of and have positive feelings and emotions about engaging in regular physical activity, (b) expect to maintain good health and improve upon their current health status, and (c) have learned proper exercise techniques. Competitive athletes, for instance, understand the expectations and requirements maintaining a high level of fitness for performing sport skills and preventing injury. In addition, for some individuals, an exercise facility, which requires a fee, is an important factor that will encourage or discourage exercise participation. Thus, income level is another factor that influences exercise behavior.

The Interpersonal

Individuals are strongly influenced by those with whom they interact. Relationships with others, interactions with persons who will both prescribe and support an exercise habit, and social support—exercising with a friend—all strongly influence exercise behavior. Physicians who inform their patients of the importance of regular physical activity, particularly when supported by data from the patient's medical examination (e.g., poor results from blood work, evidence of obesity, poor circulation, other maladies), will have a marked influence on patient exercise behavior (Pearson & Kopin, 2001). Thus, the provider-patient relationship is an important source of support for exercise behavior. Sadly, this influence has been surprisingly neglected; physicians are rarely informing their patients about the importance of exercise for improving their health. Oldridge (2001) calls for enhancing "provider adherence" by reducing the "treatment gap" between proven evidence-based, adherence-enhancing therapies and the effectiveness in which they are delivered.

The Environment

The environment in which the person lives and works dictates certain expectations and norms of "appropriate" behavior. Environmental factors provide the context in which persons participate in their personal and professional lives. Persons are more likely to exercise if they have access to equipment, facilities and transportation. Culture also influences exercise behavior. In Sweden, for example, it is normal, even expected, that most individuals will use the bicycle as a primary mode of transportation, even during elderly years. A sedentary lifestyle is more common in some cultures than others. Other environmental factors related to exercise behavior include availability, access, and transportation to fitness facilities. Taken together, these factors certainly influence a person's decision to exercise. Equally challenging is to assist individuals to entrench exercise as part of their daily schedule, thereby avoiding dropout.

In summary, there is much the MHP can do to assist clients to maintain participation in a regular exercise habit. Examples include addressing the client's motives for exercising (e.g., improve health, fitness, or physical physique, a way to meet people) and personal needs (e.g., improve confidence or self-esteem, reduce anxiety or depression, improve mood state), by providing social support (e.g., "cheerleading" your client to good health), and performance coaching to provide instruction and monitoring of progress. While only the client can create an exercise environment in which he or she feels safe, secure, and comfortable, the MHP can help clients deal with sources of worry and threat (e.g., the superior performance or physical attributes of others, overcoming fatigue and other unpleasant manifestations of training, remaining focused on goals). The ability to adhere to an exercise regimen will be a big challenge to both the MHP and to clients, but it is achievable.

STRATEGIES FOR ENHANCING EXERCISE ADHERENCE AND COMPLIANCE

Addressing the Exerciser's Dispositions

All individuals possess a set of psychological characteristics, called dispositions, which differ from more permanent, stable personality traits, that often result in certain behavioral tendencies. There are selected personal features that predict a person's willingness to begin and adhere to exercise habits. For example, a highly anxious individual is more likely to feel threatened about engaging in a program that might prove disappointing in meeting personal goals, not be able to show competence in performing exercise tasks, or may not perform certain exercises as well as others in view. The effects of these feelings on adherence is magnified when the person also is highly self-conscious (heightened awareness of how one is being perceived by others), has a high need to achieve, fears failure, sets extremely high standards, is very self-critical when these standards—which are often unrealistic—are not met (i.e., perfectionism), and has very high self-expectations of rapid success (Dunn, Anderson, & Jakicic, 1998). Competence and desirable results are expected quickly. When the reasons for exercising are based on approval from others or some other source of reward, rather than from personal enjoyment, then the person is said to be extrinsically, rather than intrinsically, motivated.

Finally, clinical issues, such as depression, social anxiety, mood disorders, eating disorders, most addictions, and the effects of medications each work toward inhibiting one's energy to commit to a permanent change in exercise habits. While it is not expected that the fitness industry employ clinical psychologists to deal with the personal issues of their members, it would be in the best interests of the exerciser to seek counseling and determine the sources of the habit of starting and then quitting new programs and of learning new skills. While there is apparently no publication that focuses on counseling issues with exercise participants, the reader is referred to a book edited by Richard Ray and Diane Weise-Bjornstal (1999) that address many of these issues in sports medicine settings.

Ensuring Perceived Success and Improvement (Intrinsic Motivation)

People are, by nature, attracted to activities that they perform well. Conversely, people tend to avoid activities that they perceive as too difficult and lead to perceived failure outcomes. The word "perceived" is important, here, because it is the individual's own interpretation of success and failure that influences continued participation, rather than an externally imposed standard or the views of others that is the indicator of competence or incompetence. Of primary concern, then, is that novice exercisers experience and gain a sense of competence—success or improvement—from their participation in exercise, however these concepts are identified to the individual. Setting realistic goals that are not too challenging at first provides a sense of comfort and security about engaging in exercise tasks that might be viewed as very challenging. The goal, then, is to give novices a sense of "can do" about their ability to engage in exercise routines successfully and with a minimum of discomfort.

Providing Instructional Feedback

Instructional feedback meets a number of needs and provides exercisers with a feeling of growth and development in exercise and social support by a specialist. There is a heightened sense of hope and optimism about overcoming physical and mental barriers (e.g., self-doubt, low confidence). Feedback also leads to improved performance quality and better results.

Ideally, the source of feedback would be data-based (quantitative), such as improved fitness test scores (e.g., minutes of aerobic exercise, pounds of resistance lifted, degrees of flexibility improved, training heart rate reached and maintained). However, qualitative feedback (e.g., positive verbal praise) is also a reliable source of improved perceived competence if the person offering the information is credible (e.g., a fitness instructor, physician, or other specialist) and the information is based on concrete, specific performance—not the usual, more general and abstract, "nice job" that lacks specificity and identifiable performance. Heightened perceptions of competence increase intrinsic motivation (a person's self-determined drive to perform a task due to feelings of competence and satisfaction).

Encouraging Social Support

While some individuals prefer to exercise alone and are highly self-motivated, others rely on friends, family members, or groups with whom to exercise or from whom to receive encouragement. Acknowledgment and approval from others often has very motivating properties. These individuals act as a primary source of motivation.

Providing Educational Materials

For many individuals, additional information about their involvement in exercise contributes to its meaningfulness and might favorably influence desirable outcomes. For example, as Gauvin and her colleagues (2001) point out, individuals who learn the benefits—psychological and physical—of exercise are more likely to adhere to their exercise habits because they feel greater control over influencing their health. Consequently, these individuals take more responsibility for maintaining their exercise regimen while anticipating the benefits. The authors also suggest that exercise specialists work with employers to develop ways to educate their workers about delivering the many benefits of exercise and other health habits. Educational materials also have high positive reinforcement value, which improves adherence, because this information provides additional, credible support for the value and desirable outcomes accrued from exercise.

Developing a Healthy Lifestyle

Finally, exercisers are more likely to adhere if their habit is ritualized as part of a new, healthy lifestyle that encompasses nutrition, stress management, and positive thoughts and emotions. Rather than an end in itself, exercise becomes a part of a new set of routines and healthy habits that improves the person's energy, facilitates a desirable change in selected dispositions (e.g., greater optimism, confidence, coping skills, reduced anxiety and other negative mood states), and improves social skills and quality of life.

Finally, Miller and colleagues (1997) make several recommendations to providers and health care organizations to increase the compliance of patients who are involved in cardiac rehabilitation exercise programs; the same recommendations have implications for healthy exercisers, too. These are:

1. Communicate clear, direct messages about the importance of a particular course of action or therapy (e.g., provide verbal and written instructions, including rationale for treatments);

2. Include patients in decisions about prevention and treatment goals (e.g., use contracting strategies, anticipate barriers to compliance and discussion solutions, negotiate goals and a plan);

3. Use behavioral strategies in the counseling process (e.g., use active listening techniques, incorporate both cognitive and behavioral strategies);

4.   Assess patient compliance at each office visit (e.g., use self-report or electronic data);

5.   Develop reminder systems to ensure identification and follow-up of the patient's status (e.g., telephone calls for follow-up); and

6.   Be proper models of good health by engaging in proper exercise and nutritional habits.

To promote compliance, health care organizations—again, with implications for the fitness center industry—should:

1.   Develop an environment that supports prevention and treatment interventions (e.g., preappointment reminders, telephone follow-up, schedule evening and weekend office hours, provide group and individual counseling for patients and their families);

2.   Provide tracking and reporting systems (e.g., develop computer-based systems to locate electronic medical records);

3.   Provide education and training for providers (e.g., require continuing education courses in communication, behavioral counseling);

4.   Encourage providers to maintain a healthy lifestyle (e.g., exercise, nutrition) in attempting to reduce the likelihood of obesity, a condition of epidemic proportions in the U.S. Providing exercise equipment at or near the worksite, or to work with exercise facilities to reduce the cost of memberships would be helpful.

5.   Provide adequate reimbursement for allocation of time for all health care professionals (e.g., develop financial incentives tied to desired patient and provider outcomes).

In summary, exercise leaders and organizations are challenged to overcome a culture that promotes the least amount of physical activity and the highest level of food intake in the world. It is imperative that the U.S. address its growing obesity epidemic, or face skyrocketing health care costs in coming years. Vastly reduced physical activity in childhood and adolescent years has not helped. Greater use of computers, more access to television alternatives, increased displeasure with participating in youth sports, and a culture obsessed with fast, high-fat food is having a detrimental effect on our health and well-being.

EXERCISE ADDICTION/DEPENDENCE

Just opposite to the problem of getting people to exercise and to adhere to their exercise habit is the person who becomes dependent on it. This concept is called exercise addiction or dependence. Originally referred to as positive addiction by Glasser (1976), the terms *exercise dependence* or *compulsion to exercise* has been more common in more recent years. Is being an exercise addict necessarily a bad thing?

While researchers and psychologists debate whether any addiction can be positive, most agree that addictions, in general, tend to be unhealthy and undesirable (Cockerill & Riddington, 1996). This is because, by definition, addictions represent behaviors that are beyond the person's control or that reflect psychopathology, such as low physique self-esteem, an eating disorder, the need for social isolation, or representing some other compensation that requires treatment (Berger et al., 2002). For example, Berger and colleagues cite other studies in which the motivation for running or weight training serves the purpose of improving body image. While it is normal to enhance one's physical features, the huge amount of time devoted to exercise, at the expense of other normal daily routines and social interactions, borders on abnormal or dysfunctional behavior. Although the compulsion to exercise may have a positive, anabolic (tissue-building) effect on the body, exercising excessively, whether it is a conscious decision or a behavioral habit driven by routine and a perceived personal need, has a catabolic (tissue-destroying) effect on the system. Negative consequences result— hence the terms *negative addiction*—such as injury, illness, social isolation, or exercising while injured or ill.

POSITIVE ADDICTION TO EXERCISE

As Glasser (1976) originally described, positive addiction is characterized by withdrawal symptoms within 24 to 36 hours without exercise. These symptoms include irritability, quick temper, anxiety, feelings of bloatedness, muscle tension, and sleeplessness. In extreme cases, the long-term cessation of regular exercise might result in changes in personal dispositions such as confidence, self-esteem, the ability to cope with stress, and self-control until the person resumes their normal exercise habits. As long as a person's exercise compulsion is *beneficial* to his or her health and psychological well-being, their exercise addiction (dependence) may be called *positive*. However, when exercise deprivation has a deleterious effect on the person's physical or mental well-being, then they have manifestations of negative addiction (dependence).

NEGATIVE ADDICTION TO EXERCISE: A MENTAL DISORDER?

The change from positive to negative exercise addiction occurs when the person becomes compulsive about their exercise routine at the exclusion of other daily activities. There are two mental conditions that likely drive a negative exercise addiction, obsessions and compulsions. According to the *Diagnostic and Statistical Manual of Mental Disorders* (1994), *obsessions* are any persistent, recurring and disturbing thought, desire, impulse, or drive that controls a person's behavior, and is viewed by the person as intrusive and inappropriate, causing significant anxiety or distress. *Compulsions* are repetitive ritualized behaviors or thoughts that persons are driven to do in order to relieve the anxiety caused by their obsessions. Obsessive-Compulsive Disorder (OCD) is present when the attempts to exert control over inner and outer worlds have become uncontrollable. One example is a person's tendency to wash his or her hands until their skin is raw in response to obsessive concerns about contamination in a distorted perception that they must stay clean. One sign of OCD is that the person is bothered by their obsessions or compulsions, and that the activities are time-consuming (typically, more than one hour a day) or interfering in the person's life.

Some individuals who suffer from negative exercise addiction feel compelled to exercise, even at the expense of working, socializing, or being involved in other important activities. Exercise is controlling their life. Thus, a negatively addicted exerciser concludes that they "must" exercise, rather than exercising for improved health, relaxation, or other forms of enjoyment, and that exercise is the center point in their life, even at the expense of their health and life satisfaction. Other manifestations of negative addiction include exercising with a serious injury, when in pain, in poor health, exercising to lose weight when, in fact, the person's weight is normal or below normal, and exercising at the expense of attending to family responsibilities or developing social relationships.

Rather than a mental disorder, exercise-deprived individuals might be exhibiting short-term disturbances in mood state and other undesirable emotions. For instance, a study conducted at the University of Wisconsin by Gregory Mondin and his colleagues (1996) examined the psychological effects of no exercise for 3 consecutive days on males and females who exercised 6 to 7 days a week for a minimum of 45 minutes per session. The researchers, using the Profile of Mood State and State-Trait Anxiety Inventory, found that decreased vigor, and simultaneous increases in tension, depression, confusion, and state anxiety occurred within 24 to 48 hours of exercise deprivation. These mood disturbances improved when exercise was resumed.

In their review of related literature, Cockerill and Riddington (1996) claim that compulsive exercisers: (a) are dissatisfied with their body or with themselves, (b) will exercise to have control, but become controlled by the activity, (c) do not enjoy having free time, (d) become dependent on the euphoric and calming benefits of exercise, (e) are avid goal-setters, and (f) become socially withdrawn. The authors claim that committed exercisers differ from their compulsive counterparts by feeling invigorated and strengthened by exercise. Compulsive exercisers, on the other hand, perceive exercise as work and no longer enjoy the pleasure that it once provided. Negatively addicted exercisers are not happy about it and require counseling.

How to Avoid Negative Exercise Addiction

Berger and colleagues (2002) provide guidelines to try to prevent negative exercise addiction. These include: (a) keeping the exercise regimen to 3 to 4 times a week, not more than 30 to 60 minutes for each bout, (b) using interval training, in which some days are harder than others, alternating high and low intensity, (c) finding a partner with whom to work out who is not obsessed with exercise, (d) scheduling rest days as part of the exercise program, (e) if injured, ensuring full recovery before starting to exercise again, and (f) setting realistic short- and long-term goals, while providing a realistic time frame to meet those goals.

Other ideas to prevent negative addiction include alternating types of exercises so that certain muscle groups are not overtrained, engaging in a balanced exercise program, including aerobic, resistance (strength), and flexibility training, including relaxation strategies in your daily routine, developing firmly entrenched health-promoting routines such as the type of exercises to be performed, the time of day they will be scheduled, and planning other activities in the day and week that promote a balanced lifestyle.

Chapter 9

Consulting With Special Populations

Walk into a fitness facility and you'll see people who are in relatively good shape, moderate to high fitness level, and free of debilitating injury or other conditions that will inhibit exercise performance. Yet, the millions of individuals with various types of physical limitations or who are not relatively fit are being underserved by the fitness industry. Clients of MHPs include individuals with various maladies, injuries, physical problems and limitations representing all age groups. All of these individuals will benefit from regular exercise; however, they will require unique exercise prescriptions and monitoring of progress. Of course, many of the conditions presented to MHPs require medical intervention, such as a doctor's clearance or working with a physical therapist or other specialist. Whereas some personal coaches are trained to administer exercise interventions to special populations the MHP is not trained to provide such information. It would be unprofessional, for instance, for the MHP to prescribe an exercise program to individuals with strict physical and medical limitations.

Nevertheless, clients trust their MHP, and the solidarity of this relationship is an important component of taking the risk of engaging in exercise. The purpose of this chapter is to provide MHPs with insights into the special needs of these populations, and how these clients often considered unhealthy or whose needs differ from the so-called "normal" adult population, can be assisted. Each of these populations will benefit markedly from regular physical activity.

REHABILITATION CLIENTS

Heart and Pulmonary Disease

Perhaps there is no population among us that is more terrified of exercise than a person who has experienced a cardiac event or has advanced cardiovascular or pulmonary disease. For these populations any activity that makes increased demands on the cardiovascular system provokes anxiety. Indeed, years ago the medical community contributed to their patients' concerns and worries by prescribing bed rest after experiencing a myocardial infarction (heart attack) or other cardiovascular events. It is now well accepted that regular physical activity reduces mortality and morbidity from cardiovascular and pulmonary disease.

There are different challenges for MHPs in fostering a positive attitude toward exercise, especially among this population. One area that requires particular attention by MHPs is returning to work, an economic and a psychosocial imperative for many cardiac patients. However, there are numerous barriers to resuming employment in this population. According to Wenger (1995), predictors of failure to return to work include the patient's perception of poor health, older age, financial disincentives, anxiety, depression, lower socioeconomic and educational status, increased job-related physical activity, low work satisfaction, and the patient's perception that his or her disease was caused by the job. Education and counseling are needed to provide accurate health status and information about the likely causes of the disease.

Regular exercise directly affects the heart by delaying the onset of atherosclerosis and reducing oxygen demands and work of the heart at rest and during submaximal exercise. Of course, exercise also improves physiological functioning and a host of other health-related benefits that will help prevent the onset of cardiovascular disease. Aerobic conditioning also improves chances of surviving a heart attack.

Clearly, the client's physician has full control over any prescription to engage in physical activity. In addition, many hospitals include extensive cardio-pulmonary exercise rehabilitation programs that include exercise physiologists, nursing staff, health psychologists, and other medical professionals that provide physiological and psychological testing and monitor the patient's progress. Most health care (insurance) programs will pay from 8 to 12 weeks of exercise rehabilitation. What, then, is the role of the MHP, given the extensive medical treatment of their client?

Clients suffering from cardiovascular and pulmonary disease need extensive psychological support and guidance, a role that the patient's physician and MHPs should provide. In a study published in the *Archives of Internal Medicine,* Ades, Waldmann, McCann, and Weaver (1992) examined the predictors of cardiac rehabilitation participation in older coronary adults. They found that "by far the most powerful predictor of participation was the strength of the primary physician's recommendation" (p. 1034). While the effectiveness of program referral by the patient's MHP has not been studied specifically, it is known that the more sources of positive social and emotional support by individuals who the patient respects the more likely the patient will engage in health-enhancing behaviors. The MHP, then, is in a unique position of offering emotional support, building confidence in the patient's ability to engage in what the patient may perceive as risky behaviors, and to overcome patient guilt in feeling helpless and dependent on family members (e.g., provide transportation, give up personal time, rearrange schedules) to accommodate the patient's medical needs.

The MHP can also provide patients with cognitive and behavioral strategies that will promote exercise adherence after the hospital rehabilitation program has been completed (see chapters 8 and 11). For example, the MHP can help clients develop favorable attitudes toward the need for improving a healthy lifestyle, to schedule exercise as part of one's daily routine, use positive self-talk at the exercise venue, and overcome intimidation and other barriers— psychological, social, and physical—that might inhibit the client from attending a fitness facility and maintaining an exercise habit. Teaching clients to use self-monitoring strategies (see Appendix A) as an instructional tool for adopting proper cognitive and behavioral strategies related to exercise preparation and performance techniques is also helpful. While the medical community retains responsibility for exercise prescriptions, instruction, and supervision, the

MHP works with the client's thoughts, emotions, and dispositions that will ignite the individual to maintain an exercise habit as a lifelong undertaking.

Injury

Most MHP clients are not competitive athletes. If they sustain an injury that results in pain until the severity of the injury is diagnosed and a physician approves engaging in physical activity, the client will not exercise. Therefore, the issues of injury severity and discomfort must first be resolved before the client is receptive to an exercise intervention. However, many individuals tend to give up after experiencing an injury, even of low severity. As one lady of about 60 years of age told me, "I just don't like the pain" that exercise brings. And although those sentiments are understandable, it is certainly in the interests of most clients to become "mentally tough" in dealing with injuries and to retain self-control of their life. Many patients will use any excuse not to become physically active and, in fact, will wrongly judge their physical condition. For example, they will use muscle stiffness, a sprained finger, or any other physical ailment as an excuse to not exercise.

What can the MHP do to motivate the individual who claims injury as the reason not to exercise? Without denying the client's honesty and integrity, the MHP can:

1. provide emotional support for the client's condition, yet express optimism about exercising in the near future;

2. remind the client of exercise benefits;

3. offer exercise alternatives such as exercising in the water, riding a stationary bicycle, resistance training, or going for a brisk walk;

4. remind the client to work on a part of the body that is free of injury or discomfort (e.g., exercising upper limbs if a leg is injured), and

5. provide referrals of individuals who might specialize in working with injured clients.

Back Problems

About 65% of the adult population suffers from mechanical low back pain, particularly in the lower lumbar region. The frequent result is loss of work, disengagement from friends and family, depression, and lower quality of life. This is serious business. Similar to the previous maladies, clients who have a bad back need professional consulting from their physician or physical therapist prior to engaging in an exercise program. For many clients, the only means of exercise is through the clinic of a physical therapist or chiropractor. However, the MHP can also make a contribution toward encouraging inactive clients to engage in as much physical activity as they can within the confines of their medical condition.

No one has a monopoly of experiencing back pain. While both genders suffer back pain at a similar rate, women are more vulnerable as a result of pregnancy. Men more then women, however, store excess body fat in the abdominal area. Abdominal fat (i.e., "the beer gut" or "paunch") results in a hyperflexion of the low back—the lumbar vertebrae—in which the discs between the vertebrae are in a constant state of compression. A painful low back is the result. This explains the frequency with which pregnant women experience low back pain. It is important, therefore, that persons with low back pain strengthen their abdominal muscles and attempt to reduce the amount of accumulated fat in the abdominal area.

Primary Causes of Back Pain

1. *Large abdominal area.* As just discussed, excessive fat accumulation in the abdominal region results in a hyperextension of the lumbar vertebrae that puts pressure on the discs between each vertebra, causing pain. Strengthening abdominal muscles and reducing abdominal fat are proper behavioral techniques to help stop low back discomfort.

2. *Poor body mechanics.* We often move in a manner that is contrary to proper mechanics, placing added strain on our back. Bending from the waist to lift an object, especially with knees straight, is an example. To lift an object, bend at the knees. Leg muscles should do most of the work. In addition, the

object being lifted should be kept close to the body, abdominal muscles should be tightened, and the back straight.

3. *Poor flexibility.* Tight hamstring muscles—located behind the thigh—also contribute to back pain. Hamstring muscles keep the pelvis from "rolling forward" as you bend forward. The inability of the pelvis to roll forward will cause increased stress on the low back. Slow stretching of the hamstrings will help relieve this problem.

4. *Poor posture.* Observe how most of us sit in a chair or work with our computer, for example. Our back tends to be unsupported because of poor posture. Poor posture is often unconscious and we tend not to be aware of it. Poor posture stretches muscle groups out of position reducing their work potential and causing other muscles to work harder. The key to maintaining good posture is strengthening those muscles responsible for supporting the pelvis. The goal is to tilt the pelvis upward and backward, thus reducing the curve in the low back. When the pelvis is level and the curve of the low back is reduced or slightly flat, the back is at its strongest and symptoms of pain and discomfort often disappear.

   To flatten the curve in the low back: (a) Increase the flexibility and mobility of the pelvic area; (b) strengthen the abdominal, gluteal, and back muscles; and (c) slowly stretch and lengthen tight muscles and other structures in the low back.

The key role of the MHP for clients with back discomfort is to help them replace taking a plethora of pain drugs with behavioral approaches. Examples include slow, deliberate movements, exercising in a safe environment (e.g., in the water, on a stationary bicycle, yoga, abdominal exercises), and to build daily rituals that lead to regular bouts of physical activity. From a mental perspective, MHPs can help clients build the necessary confidence and self-control that allows the client to take back control of their health and of their life. MHPs know that many clients engage in a coping technique called catastrophizing, common among individuals who feel helpless and are experiencing discomfort. Catastrophizing consists of complaining and feelings of helplessness and extreme anxiety due to perceptions of low self-control in a given situation (American Psychiatric Association, 1994). Instead, the MHP wants to help clients to replace negative self-talk, thoughts of self-pity, and low self-esteem with a "can do" attitude about engaging in healthy behaviors. Then clients are ready to be sent to a physical therapist or other specialist to teach them proper exercise techniques.

EXERCISE FOR DIABETICS

Diabetes mellitus is a disease in which the body fails to produce or properly respond to insulin. Insulin is a hormone needed to convert sugars, starches, and other foods into energy. These food substances are converted during digestion into glucose, which is an energy fuel source. If a person lacks insulin, glucose cannot enter body cells where it can be utilized as an energy source. Instead, glucose will accumulate in the bloodstream causing hyperglycemia (high blood sugar). If left untreated, hyperglycemia may lead to cardiovascular disease, blindness, amputations, and damage to the liver, kidney, and nerves. Clearly, approval by a physician is needed before a client diagnosed with diabetes begins an exercise program.

Benefits and Possible Problems for the Exercising Diabetic

There are significant benefits for a diabetic to engage in an exercise program. First, since diabetics tend to be overweight or obese—which could have caused the diabetic condition in the first place, or was a reaction (i.e., overeating) to the disease—exercise will likely lead to improved weight control. In addition, because muscle cells use glucose from the bloodstream, glucose level will decrease due to exercise; glucose is required to fuel physical activity.

There are, however, a couple of possible problems associated with diabetes and exercise. First, the lack of sufficient insulin may induce hyperglycemia (high blood sugar) due to decreased cellular absorption of glucose. Therefore, diabetics who require insulin should exercise only when their blood glucose level (or peak insulin activity) is above 240 mg/dl.

The second potential problem is the hypoglycemic (low blood sugar) effect that occurs with injected insulin, particularly if the injection was administered into the exercising muscle, for instance, a runner's thigh. The insulin is absorbed into the exercising muscle more quickly because of increased circulation, improving the likelihood that blood sugar (blood glucose) will drop. To avoid a hypoglycemic reaction, the diabetic should not exercise during the "peak time" of the prescribed insulin. In addition, because exercise itself has an insulin-like effect, the insulin-dependent diabetic should either reduce insulin dosage or increase the intake of carbohydrates.

Exercise Guidelines

Recommendations for prescribing exercise to a person with diabetes include the following:

1. Exercise 1–2 hours after a meal, not before. This is when the blood sugar level is rising. Have a pre-exercise snack 15–20 minutes before activity begins and during prolonged exercise bouts. In addition, for each 30 minutes of activity a 10 g carbohydrate snack (e.g., fruit, fruit juice) is recommended.

2. To promote exercise adherence, participate in activities that are enjoyable. Develop rituals that induce exercise behavior such as planned exercise sessions at particular times and venues, having an exercise plan, and obtaining performance coaching to ensure proper exercise technique.

3. Eat food that metabolizes slowly such as protein to prevent low blood sugar. Rapidly available simple carbohydrates include raisins and candy, but use sparingly before and after an exercise session (again, a physical should be consulted to determine individual needs).

4. Carry an identification card and, if possible, exercise with a partner that will recognize symptoms of hyperglycemia and who knows where your carbohydrate source is carried.

5. Wear properly fitting shoes and inspect your feet for blisters before and after any physical activity, even if the activity consists of a leisure stroll. For the diabetic, a blister, if left untreated, can become a source of serious medical problems, including amputation.

6. Social support, that is, encouragement from others or exercising with others should be encouraged. Diabetics, often

because of weight control problems, will find exercise to be a challenge, physically and emotionally.

7. Attempt to reach your target heart rate by calculations offered in chapter 6.

8. Stress reduction will decrease hypertension, which facilitates blood transport to all tissues.

9. Similar to recommendations to overweight individuals, diabetics will find low impact or water aerobic activity best suited for their condition.

EXERCISE FOR CHILDREN

Children are at particular risk of becoming obese and developing various diseases, most notably type 2 diabetes, due to an inactive lifestyle that includes ingesting far too many calories. Most health agencies recommend that children older than age 6 years accumulate at least 30 minutes of moderately intense exercise on most, if not all, days of the week. In young children, the emphasis should be on active play, while older children should be encouraged to exercise 20–30 minutes at least 3 times per week. All forms of physical activity should emphasize enjoyment; the operational term is "fun" when helping your child clients become more physically active. It is less necessary for children than adults to monitor their heart rate response during exercise because they are at low cardiac risk and can adjust their exercise intensity according to tolerance and their own perception of exertion (Rowland, 2005).

Is exercise safe for children? Will it stunt growth? The concept of harmful effects of exercise on growth in young children was derived years ago from animal studies and, more recently, from research on possible growth stunting effects from intense training among female gymnasts (Rowland, 2005). However, Rowland has concluded from his extensive review of this literature "it is accepted that increased physical activity and musculoskeletal stress are important for *promoting* [his italics] growth in children. Moreover, children's involvement in sport training might provide particular long-term health benefits (e.g., stimulation of bond growth and density may ameliorate the risk of future osteoporosis)" (p. 33).

What about resistance training? Should children lift weights to promote muscular strength? Again, "old thinking"—circa the late 1970's—was that strength development is closely related to sexual maturation, thus, strength training can only be effective in the post-pubertal age." More recently, according to Rowland (2005), "The accumulated research . . . indicates quite convincingly that both pre-pubertal girls and boys are, in fact, capable of improving strength with a period of resistance training" (p. 199). It is true, however, that children do not generally develop muscle hypertrophy while gaining strength during resistance training due to a lack of testosterone. Nevertheless, moderate resistance training is desirable for children and adolescents.

Exercise Guidelines

These guidelines come from the American Council of Sports Medicine (ACSM, 2001).

1.   Exercise should involve large muscle groups and include weight-bearing activity. This will develop aerobic fitness, bone health, and help control weight.

2.   Children should participate in a variety of activities. If possible, both aerobic and resistance (strength) training should be incorporated into the child's exercise regimen. As MHPs know, as kids enter preadolescence, they become far more aware of their physique (i.e., physique self-esteem). This is when resistance training exercise becomes more meaningful. However, building muscle should not be at the expense of cardiovascular fitness, which burns more calories per minute than any other type of activity.

3.   Be careful of kids who rely on organized youth sport as their only form of activity. The child involved in a single sport, for example, is in danger of burning out from physical activity. The sport-addicted youngster also has to overcome perfectionistic coaches (and sometimes parents) who train their athletes much too hard. Exercise burnout is one reason former athletes refuse to exercise.

4.   All strength training should be supervised. There is a proper way to lift weights, and improper techniques can cause injury.

5.   Proper breathing in strength training is essential. Exhaling and never holding one's breath should always accompany lifting.

6.   A slow control speed is important to all exercises.

7.   Power lifting and body building during childhood and adolescence should be avoided. It's far too strenuous for these age groups and may cause injury. No matter how big and strong the individual appears he or she is not physically mature.

8.   Recommended:

Frequency: 2 times per week

Intensity: A resistance level should be selected so that the individual can perform at least 8 repetitions with proper technique.

Duration: 1–2 sets, 1–10 different exercises (8–12 repetitions)

9.   *Safety Concerns:* Safety for children should be a primary concern of all adults, including MHPs. Children are susceptible to higher incidences of overuse injuries or damage to the bone plates if exercise is too excessive. Whenever children begin new activities, they should start slow and progress slowly. Special attention should also be given to exercising in hot environments. Children do not dissipate their heat as well as adults because of a slower rate of sweating and a greater production of heat per pound of body weight. In addition, children also lose heat faster than adults in cold environments, thereby increasing the risk of hypothermia.

EXERCISE FOR THE ELDERLY

This age group will form a significant segment of the population as the baby boomers reach retirement age. MHPs will be seeing more and more clients over the age of 60 in coming years. Far too many elderly perceive the unpleasant aspects of aging (e.g., decreased cognitive and physiological processes, medical disabilities) as inevitable. The consequence is excessive reliance on drugs to combat age-related conditions, while ignoring the exercise option as a way to prevent or overcome these problems. The important point here is that there's a difference between chronological age and physiological age. Here's some good news for all of us: According to several studies, the aging process in both physiological and cognitive forms, can be slowed markedly through regular aerobic activity.

Before providing exercise guidelines for this age group, it is important to note that older adults vary significantly, more so than younger adults, in their health status and fitness level. We all age at different rates and possess various physical limitations and exercise interests. Therefore, ACSM (2001) recommends an individual approach to exercise prescription. Finally, it is essential that elderly participants receive medical clearance before engaging in vigorous exercise.

Exercise Guidelines

1.   Types of exercises include brisk walking and exercising in the water (e.g., water aerobics, stationary or regular bicycling, swimming) so that pressure to the skeletal system is minimal.

2.   The activity should be enjoyable and conveniently located—the elderly tend not to drive.

3.   The elderly, perhaps more than most age groups, prefer physical activities in social, or group, settings. This will promote safety and adherence to the activity.

4.   Other forms of activities appropriate for this age group include yard work, climbing stairs, and recreational activities. While golf and fishing are popular recreational pursuits, they rarely provide an exercise effect because the individual remains sedentary.

5.   Recommended:

> *Intensity:* Start slow and progress according to tolerance and preference.

Duration: Exercise does not have to be continuous to produce benefits. Increasing duration rather than intensity is preferred to avoid injury.

Frequency: Exercise at a low to moderate intensity should be completed most days of the week. However, exercising at a greater intensity should be performed at least three times per week on alternative days, such as Monday, Wednesday, and Friday.

    6.   Resistance training, in addition to cardiovascular fitness, is very important. Lifting weights helps to minimize the loss of muscle strength and improves the stability of joints. Favorable results include reduced chance of injury and improved movement flexibility. All exercises should be performed in a slow, controlled manner using a maximum range of motion so that the person can achieve without discomfort. For the elderly, in particular, resistance machines are recommended over free weights because machines require less skill to use and are more easily controlled (ACSM, 2001).

EXERCISE FOR PREGNANT WOMEN

Many years ago it was thought that women who were inactive or sedentary before conception should not begin an exercise program. More recent recommendations, however, encourage all pregnant women to engage in low to moderate activity such as walking or swimming. Exercise is viewed by the medical community as good for the health of pregnant women. However, it is imperative that the woman's physician provides clearance and guidance about the types and intensity level of exercise she can perform. This is because pregnancy changes a woman's physiology. Heart rate and stroke volume increase, both at rest and during exercise. Basal metabolism rate (BMR)—the number of calories burned to sustain life while at rest—increases during pregnancy. The stage of pregnancy and the fetus's condition are other issues that help determine the nature of a woman's exercise regimen. Still controversial is whether prolonged, intense jumping, common in advanced aerobic dance classes, contributes to miscarriage. A woman's personal physician should be consulted on this issue.

Reasons to Stop Exercising and Seek Medical Attention

Of course, pregnancies can be complicated and have a very serious affect on a woman's health. If the following symptoms are experienced, the pregnant woman should seek medical attention immediately:

- Signs of bloody discharge from the vagina;

- Amniotic fluid leakage;

- Sudden swelling of the ankles, hands, or face;

- Swelling or pain in the calf (a condition called phlebitis);

- Severe headaches;

- Dizziness;

- Chest pain;

- Preterm labor; or

- Decreased fetal movement.

Exercise Guidelines

1. Exercise choices should be enjoyable. Popular forms of exercise include brisk walking and water exercise.

2. It is best to avoid exercises or sports with sudden starts and stops, straining joints, ligaments, and muscles, or sports that increase the risk of falling or of blows to the abdomen with a ball. Examples include racquetball, softball, basketball, downhill skiing, soccer.

3. Recommended:

Intensity: Regular exercise using the normal training heart rate formula of 220 − age × .60 (or .70 for more active individuals)

Frequency: 3–4 times per week

Duration: 20–40 minutes (however, the duration should be based on how the woman feels; exercise should stop before she feels fatigued).

4. After the first trimester exercise in the supine position (i.e., while on the back) should be avoided. This position enlarges the uterus that can apply pressure to the blood vessels and limit blood flow.

5. Avoid exercising in the heat. Hypothermia may induce fetal distress and birth abnormalities. Always stay well hydrated; drink plenty of fluids (preferably water) before, during, and after exercise (not diuretics such as drinks with caffeine).

6. Avoid overstretching or making movements that change direction rapidly.

7. Avoid holding the breath during resistance training. Intensity level should be kept low to moderate to allow 12–15 repetitions without fatigue.

8. Watch for warning signs or symptoms that something feels "wrong." Stop exercising immediately when not feeling well.

9. Finally, if there is a lack of history of exercising regularly, avoid suddenly training for a marathon. Take it slow and allow the body to adjust to a gradual increase in physical demands.

OBESITY

With about 63% of adults in the U.S. diagnosed as overweight or obese, this is a particularly important area of intervention for MHPs. A client whose body weight is excessive may reflect a host of psychological issues that need clinical intervention. The psychological conditions clients present to the MHP may impede his or her readiness to commit to an exercise program. Many individuals will indicate their willingness to exercise after losing weight. Of course, that (i.e., losing weight, then starting an exercise program) rarely happens. It is important, therefore, that exercise should be *an integral part* of the client's therapy, not merely follow it.

Before suggesting strategies for helping overweight clients to begin an exercise program, it is important to review a very important study conducted by Steven Blair and Suzanne Brodney from the Cooper Institute in Dallas that was published in *Medicine & Science in Sports & Exercise* in 1999. The study reviewed the results of 24 studies concerning the influence of exercise on several parameters of health among four groups, active and inactive normal weight adults and active and inactive obese individuals. The primary research question is, "Does exercise have similar or even superior physiological benefits to health (morbidity and mortality) among obese individuals as it does among normal weight persons?" In other words, is exercise a bigger factor to overall health than weight? Will obese individuals who engage in regular exercise accrue similar health benefits as their normal weight counterparts, or as compared to normal weight persons who are sedentary? The results were surprising. The researchers concluded:

> Regular physical activity clearly attenuates many of the health risks associated with overweight or obesity; (2) physical activity appears to not only attenuate the health risks of overweight and obesity, but active obese individuals actually have lower morbidity and mortality than normal weight individuals who are sedentary, and (3) inactivity and low cardiorespiratory fitness are as important as overweight and obesity as mortality predictors. (Blair & Brodney, 1999, p. S646)

Thus, irrespective of a person's body weight, exercise can have significant health benefits. Weight, then, should not be the criterion on which we judge whether or not to exercise or to *continue* exercising just because significant weight loss is not quickly apparent. Being physically active is of crucial importance to good health, no matter the person's body weight.

Exercise Guidelines

Here are some exercise strategies MHPs should consider when working with overweight clients.

1. Use the Disconnected Values Intervention Model in chapter 10. The model fosters the idea that we are driven by our values, and that the negative habits we bring to our daily routines, such as no exercise, is disconnected from the values of health, family (i.e., we want to remain healthy for the people we love and who love us), performance excellence, and others. Whether this disconnect is acceptable to clients is the key issue concerning

their motivation to replace the negative habit with the positive routine of regular exercise.

2.   Overweight people often have a body image concern. Thus, exercising in a fitness facility inhabited with fitter, leaner, often younger individuals may be intimidating. Unless the individual feels comfortable in that setting, perhaps exercising with a friend, this may not be the place to recommend. Home fitness equipment is fine, however, it often sits unused after a brief time because we associate home with relaxation and do not incorporate exercise into our home environment and schedule. Work out a plan with clients that includes when (i.e., days of the week and hour of the day), and where (e.g., home, fitness club, work environment) they will exercise, and develop mental readiness strategies (e.g., getting psyched up, being enthusiastic and positive). Using the Self-Monitoring Checklist (Appendix A) is also advised.

3.   Remind clients to start slow. It took years of inactivity to reach their current fitness level and physical features, so allow time to pass before there's change in fitness, reduced effort due to training, and physical appearance.

4.   Be careful about clients' exercise selections. Overweight individuals should not jog; it's too hard on the lower limbs. Brisk walking, stationary bicycle riding, water exercise, and resistance training are examples of exercise that will not likely induce injury.

5.   Personal coaching is particularly valuable to unfit, overweight individuals. They need to start slow and not try to "catch up" to become fit and reduce weight too quickly. On the other hand, many novice exercisers—normal weight and overweight—move too slowly to reach a training effect. Brisk walking, not strolling, with interval training that combines rapid with slow movement intervals (e.g., 3 minutes higher intensity, 3 minutes reduced intensity over 20–30 minutes) is an example of a good exercise plan for novices.

6.   Remind clients to never use food as a reward for exercising. Just because they exercised does not mean they have "earned" the right to eat more or have dessert today.

7.   Do not allow your clients to rely on diet at the expense of not exercising, a common habit and myth among individuals who want to lose weight. Their reliance on diet rather than physical activity has no doubt failed them in the past and will continue to fail them. One main reason for this is due to marked changes in their basal metabolic rate (BMR)—the body's energy expenditure while at rest. According to MacKinnon and colleagues (2003), "Weight loss through diet but without exercise causes BMR to decline by up to 15 to 20%, partially because of loss of muscle mass and an apparent increase in metabolic efficiency that is, the body uses less energy for normal functions" (p. 166). In other words, reliance on dieting without exercise results in *fewer* calories burned per minute at rest. Metabolism slows down.

8.   Your client should be combining sensible eating habits with physical activity if weight loss is desirable. Late night eating (and alcohol intake) significantly contribute to weight gain. Eating several small meals during the day is clearly superior.

9.   Whether or not your client loses weight, exercise should continue as its own goal.

10.   Increase your client's daily activities beyond their exercise session. Examples include walking whenever possible and taking the stairs instead of the elevator or escalator.

11.   Be sure your clients include both cardiovascular and resistance training as part of their fitness regimen. Cardiovascular exercise results in burning more calories per minute and improved physiological functioning more than any other type of activity. Resistance training will build muscle tissue that increases BMR.

In summary, the overweight or obese individual is in great need of physical activity. Their rate of disease and premature death will be markedly higher than the rest of the population. There are many factors that have prevented them from exercising regularly and gaining considerable weight, and those factors—perhaps psychopathological in nature—should be treated clinically in conjunction with their exercise regimen. Exercise is a behavioral strategy in the process of weight loss and should be considered an integral part of treatment.

Chapter 10

A Proposed Values-Based Model for Promoting Exercise Behavior

THE NEED FOR A NEW INTERVENTION MODEL TO PROMOTE EXERCISE BEHAVIOR

Existing models do not adequately explain nor predict the causes of a person's choice not to exercise or to discontinue (nonadhere to) their exercise habit (Buckworth & Dishman, 2002). It is known that positive attitudes toward exercise and knowledge about the benefits of exercise are insufficient in promoting a permanent exercise habit. Correlations between knowledge and attitude about exercise are moderate, however, neither significantly predict actual exercise *behavior*. One likely reason for the lack of predictability is that interventions have tended to be imposed on the individual, and that researchers have not controlled for the exerciser's motives, rationale, and personal commitment to begin and maintain an exercise program. Instead, as is the common protocol in experimental research, intervention studies have consisted of volunteers who are healthy, unfit, and not currently exercising regularly.

One area, virtually ignored by researchers who study exercise interventions, has been creating a climate and providing intervention content that includes a sense of purpose, that is, "the energy derived from connecting to deeply held values and a purpose beyond one's self-interest" (Loehr & Schwartz, 2003, p. 131). The authors explain self-destructive behaviors and negative habits (e.g., poor nutrition, lack of exercise, high stress) as reflecting a "lack of . . . firm beliefs and compelling values (that are) easily buffeted by the prevailing winds. If we lack a strong sense of purpose (i.e., what really matters to us; our passion) we cannot hold our ground when we are challenged by life's inevitable storms" (p. 133). As discussed later, taking into account a person's values and beliefs forms a foundation on which future intervention research is needed.

The extant exercise intervention literature has serious limitations that, taken together, lend credence to the present model. First, previous studies examining ways to promote exercise participation and adherence have addressed specific cognitive (e.g., positive self-talk, imagery, cognitive appraisal) and behavioral strategies (e.g., goal setting, music, social support), rather than a coherent intervention program. Second, previous intervention research has focused on outcomes, for example, changes in attitude toward exercise and level of exercise adherence. Not addressed is the process by which improvements in exercise behavior occur. For instance, providing educational materials, personal coaching, and social support may, either combined or separately, improve adherence—temporarily, at least. However, unknown are the mechanisms (i.e., the personal, situational, and environmental issues) that lead to behavior changes.

One such likely mechanism is what Oldridge (2001) refers to as "regimen factors" to improve adherence. Oldridge acknowledges, "strategies for improving adherence, with long-term interventions are seldom very effective on their own" (p. 332). However, if the strategies are implemented as an integral part of one's daily routine, adherence is far more likely. In particular, he suggests "keeping the regimen straightforward, providing clear instructions and periodic checks, promoting good communication with the patient, and reinforcing their accomplishments" (p. 322). Thus, an intervention model is needed that lends support to these suggestions.

A third limitation of previous intervention research is the lack of personal involvement in voluntarily choosing (i.e., perceived choice) and committing to the type and schedule of exercise involvement. Typically, exercisers are required to attend group sessions, often at specific times, performing predetermined exercise routines. The absence from these sessions have often operationally defined nonadherence. There has been relatively little attention given, however, to allowing participants to select their own exercise regimen, venue, and schedule.

In their extensive critique of previous intervention research, Buckworth and Dishman (2002) claim "many interventions have been developed without a theoretical model or with only selected components of a model." In addition, "interventions are typically not tested to see whether they change the variables they are designed to change, or whether the target variables are actually responsible for changes in the outcome variable" (p. 252). As Glasgow, Klesges, Dzewaltowski, Bull, and Estabrooks (2004) have concluded from their review of the extant health behavior research, "it is well documented that the results of most behavioral and health promotion studies have not been translated into practice" (p. 3).

Three other cognitions that have received considerably more attention in descriptive (i.e., predicting exercise behavior) than experimental (exercise intervention) research includes perceived control, perceived competence, and exercise self-efficacy. *Perceived control* over one's health (Wallston, Smith, & King, 1983), *perceived competence* in performing exercise techniques and in meeting fitness goals (Markland, 1999), and *exercise self-efficacy* (Treasure & Newbery, 1998) have each been studied with respect to describing exercise initiation and adherence. Not surprisingly, exercise adherence is more likely when individuals feel heightened self-determination over their decision to exercise, to select the type of exercise regimen, and feel confident in reaching their exercise goals. However, although the presence of each of these cognitions are likely to produce improved participation rates, the extent to which each of these factors may be manipulated to affect exercise participation and adherence rates is less certain.

Perhaps the most widespread area neglected by researchers in attempting to increase exercise behavior is the failure to take into account the individual's *values and beliefs* about what they consider important. Unless the person endorses values such as health, family, and performance excellence that are consistent with a healthy and active lifestyle, their willingness to begin and maintain an exercise program is unlikely. As Ockene (2001) correctly concludes, "change is a process, not a one-time event, and we can't expect people to make changes at a level for which they're not ready. Our interventions need to be directed to where the individual is" (p. 45). Values, then, form the foundation of the present model.

The Importance of Values in Promoting Exercise

Values are core beliefs that guide behavior, provide impetus for motivating behavior, and provide standards against which we assess behavior (Rokeach, 1973). Values are highly relevant to establishing a person's individuality and help our understanding of behavior. For example, as Rokeach contends, a person who values health will tend to develop daily rituals and long-term habits that enhance health and general well being. According to Hogan and Mookherjee (1981), "values may be one of the most distinguishing characteristics motivating human beings and the likely effects of values on human behavior, beliefs, and attitudes are indisputable" (p. 29).

Crace and Hardy (1997) developed an eight-step values-based intervention to enhance sports team building. Briefly, their model consists of:

1. helping athletes understand the importance of individual differences for enhanced performance (i.e., it's ok to have differences in team member personality);

2. assessing individual differences on the athletes' own goals and values;

3. understanding the interactions between values and life roles (i.e., values are identified within each life role),

4. identifying and understanding the primary team values (i.e., values shared by team members),

5. identifying ways in which values can enhance or inhibit team cohesion (e.g., the athlete's value of responsibility can improve commitment to team success, but can also result in being overwhelmed by the lack of responsibility from selected teammates, resulting in mental fatigue and guilt),

6. developing an action plan to improve compatibility of the athletes' and the team's values with the ultimate purpose of improving attainment of team values,

7. performing similar athlete and team strategies with the team's coaches, and finally,

8. scheduling follow-up meetings with the athletes and coaches to discuss the effectiveness of the team-building program.

The strength of this model is the recognition that a person's values guide his or her behavior, and that sharing values with others has a strong effect on the commitment to sacrifice personal, self-serving needs for the benefit of others, in this case, the team. With respect to developing and keeping an exercise habit, the model suggests avoiding self-indulgence that leads to poor health, and fostering habits, such as exercise and proper nutrition, that benefit family and friends—the people who love us.

Values alone, however, cannot induce behavior change. Values are more central determinants of behavior than are interests and attitudes (Super, 1995), the latter of which are more situational and derived from a core set of values. Thus, a plethora of interests and attitudes are derived from a relatively reduced number of values. In addition, interests, attitudes, and needs are transitory, once satiated, may not influence behavior. Values, on the other hand, are almost always firmly entrenched and stable, therefore, transcend situations and guide behavior over a long period of time.

While research on values and exercise behavior is lacking, it is plausible to surmise that values predict behavior (Brown & Crace, 1996; Hogan & Mookherjee, 1981). Thus, individuals who value health are more likely to engage in behaviors that enhance their health. If family is an important value, than predictably, more time and effort will be devoted toward enhancing family relationships and well-being. However, if health forms part of a person value system, and the individual's behaviors are inconsistent with this value (e.g., not exercising, poor nutrition, lack of sleep), the link between value and behavior is disconnected. This "disconnect" forms an important segment of the current model to initiate exercise behavior.

To what extent does a person value their health and happiness, as opposed to how much effort and time they put into it? For exercisers, expect there to be a high degree of consistency between the person's stated importance about their health and the time they invest in it. For sedentary individuals who state that their health is important, however, expect to see a large discrepancy. Many individuals say they value their health (and happiness), however, the amount of time they put into improving and maintaining good health may not reflect this value. This is called a *disconnect*, and forms the basis for helping individuals change their exercise behavior.

There are a host of barriers, mostly psychological, that explains the absence of a regular exercise routine in the lives of many people. Realistically, engaging in physical activity at the correct level of intensity, duration, and frequency to obtain sufficient health and medical benefits is simply too unpleasant for many people. We pay a heavy price for leading an inactive lifestyle. These individuals conclude that the "benefits" of remaining sedentary and not exercising (e.g., having more time to do other things, not experiencing the discomfort associated with vigorous exercise) are greater than the "costs" of remaining sedentary (e.g., weight gain, poorer health, reduced lifespan). Perhaps, only when these costs are greater than the benefits, and that the person perceives the costs as unacceptable, will there be the proper "ignition" to begin and maintain an exercise habit. I have produced a model (Figure 10.1) that shows the role of a person's deepest values and beliefs about whether or not to begin and maintain an exercise habit. Let's review the model.

SPIRITUAL FITNESS: LINKING VALUES TO EXERCISE HABITS

Dr. Jack Groppel (2000), in his book, *The Corporate Athlete*, has a very interesting perspective on the way to ignite an individual's desire to start and maintain an exercise program. He calls it "spiritual fitness," and it is totally unrelated to religious practice. To Groppel, spirituality involves moral, ethical, and (perhaps) religious attitudes, feelings, and values. Loehr and Schwartz (2003) include a spirituality component in their corporate program in attempting to get corporate clients to change habits that negatively affect health and quality of work. The authors define spiritual capacity as "the energy that is unleashed by tapping into one's deepest values and defining a strong sense of purpose" (p. 127). This capacity, they claim, "serves as sustenance in the face of adversity and as a powerful source of motivation, focus, determination, and resilience" (p. 127).

The individual is asked probing, personal questions, such as "to what extent are your values consistent with your actions? If you

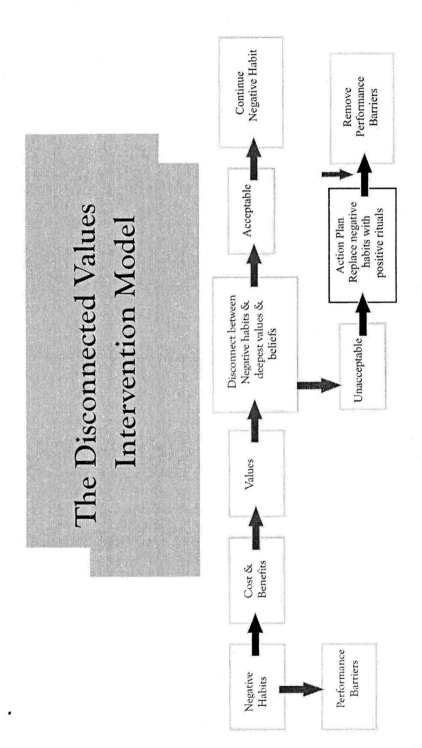

The Disconnected Values Intervention Model

- Continue Negative Habit
- Acceptable
- Disconnect between Negative habits & deepest values & beliefs
- Values
- Cost & Benefits
- Negative Habits
- Performance Barriers
- Unacceptable
- Action Plan Replace negative habits with positive rituals
- Remove Performance Barriers

FIGURE 10.1   The Disconnected Values Model (DVM).

137

value your health, for instance, do you have habits that are not good for you, and therefore, inconsistent with your values? What about your family? Do you value your spouse, children, or parents? If you lead a sedentary lifestyle and are not involved in a program of exercise, yet one of your deepest values is to maintain good health, to what extent is your value inconsistent with your behavior? Is there a 'disconnect' between your beliefs about good health and your unhealthy behavioral patterns?"

Groppel also asks us to determine the "benefits" of our negative habits, such as lack of exercise (e.g., more time to do other things, not experiencing the discomfort of physical exertion, fitness club membership costs), and then to identify the costs of our sedentary lifestyle (e.g., weight gain, reduced mental health, low physique self-esteem, higher level of "bad" cholesterol). Are these costs acceptable? If they are, then the negative habit (i.e., lack of exercise, in this case) will likely continue. However, if the costs and long-term consequences are far greater than the benefits, and the person finds these costs unacceptable, than a change in behavior is far more likely. Groppel calls this process expanding spiritual capacity.

THE DISCONNECTED VALUES MODEL (DVM)

As indicated earlier, the process of behavior change is a challenging process because habits and routines, in this case, lack of regular exercise, is firmly entrenched in the person's lifestyle (Ockene, 2001). Attempting to increase exercise behavior is particularly difficult because it is accompanied by an array of long-held feelings and attitudes that may reflect negative previous experiences (e.g., the physical education teacher who used exercise as a form of discipline, burnout from too much physical training as a former athlete, injury from previous exercise attempts). Further, vigorous exercise requires effort and some degree of physical discomfort in order to obtain the well-known benefits. The degree of discomfort, often measured as "ratings of perceived exertion" (Borg, 1998) is directly related to the extent to several criteria such as current body weight, the extent of poor fitness, the degree to which the person's lifestyle is sedentary. Thus, a new approach for effective intervention outcomes is needed. Figure 10.1 illustrates the Disconnected Values Model (DVM).

The DVM is predicated on two postulates that define self-motivated behavior that have strong implications toward promoting exercise, both of which are often missing from existing exercise intervention research. The first postulate is that self-motivated behavior reflects a person's deepest values and beliefs about his or her passion, that is, the "power of purpose" (Loehr & Schwartz, 2003). Purpose prompts the desire to become fully engaged in activities that "really matter" in meeting personal goals and future aspirations. The second postulate is that the primary motivators of normal human behavior are: (a) to identify a deeply held set of values, (b) to live a life consistent with those values, and (c) to consistently hold ourselves accountable to them. Thus, ostensibly, an individual whose values include health, family, and performance excellence—to name three common values should be self-motivated to exercise because it is consistent with these values. A deeper sense of purpose consists of shifting one's attention from fulfilling one's own needs and desires to serving and meeting the needs of others. An exerciser who values family, for instance, realizes that they will have more energy and lead a higher quality of life in meeting the needs of friends and family members. Perhaps, then, the self-motivated drive to develop an exercise habit rests, at least in part, on recognizing the inconsistency between one's negative habits (i.e., lack of regular exercise) and their values, and then to institute a new, positive habit of exercise that is strongly connected to one's values. As Loehr and Schwartz (2003) conclude, "deeply held values fuel the energy on which purpose is built" (p. 140).

The DVM is based on the interaction between the MHP and his or her client over a period of a few sessions. It reflects receiving information, self-reflection, and ultimately, self-determination about acknowledging the truth about current behaviors, the feelings and emotions that underlie those behaviors, determining the person's goals, and finally, identifying the strategies needed to reach those goals. The model does not consist of a pre-determined set of cognitive and behavioral strategies, although strategies may embellish the person's action plan in carrying out the intervention.

Negative Habits

The model begins by acknowledging the existence of negative habits, defined as thoughts, emotions, or tasks we experience regularly that we know are not healthy or in our best interests, yet, remain under our control. Despite our ability to prevent or stop these negative habits, we continue to experience them. In this example, not exercising and poor nutrition form negative habits that need changing. The result, seen in Table 10.1, is low energy, premature mental and physical fatigue, poor health, excessive weight, and reduced quality of life.

TABLE 10.1   Examples of Negative Habits That Cause or Explain Performance Barriers

Physical Barriers	Emotional Barriers	Cognitive Barriers	Spiritual Barriers
Lack of sleep	Poor communication	Self-critical	Lack of passion
Smoking	Impatience	Multitasking	Low need to achieve
Poor nutrition	Anger/hostility	Inflexible	Lack of empathy/ compassion
Sedentary lifestyle	Pessimism	Poor mental preparation	Abuse of power
Excessive alcohol or caffeine	Chronic state anxiety	Defensive	"Me first" attitude
Poor hydration	Bullied by others	Poor time management	No focus (mission) in life
Low energy and fatigue	Poor coping skills	Rigid/inflexible	Disconnected with passions in life
Unkempt physical appearance	Lack of assertiveness	Poor work/life balance	Rarely gives credit or praises others
	Sarcastic	Impatience	Lacks proper values
	Persistent conflict with supervisor and others	Poor organization	Lack of desirable family relationships
	Driven by guilt	No respect for others	
	Chronic anxiety	Poor decision making (lacks speed and accuracy)	
	Poor coping skills	Poor time management	
	Driven by fear and insecurity	Lack of concentration	
		Mental fatigue	
		Lack of trust in others	
		Low self-control	

Performance Barriers

Performance barriers are operationally defined as a persistent thought, emotion, or action that compromises and creates obstacles to high-quality performance. Whether these barriers are actual (e.g., injury, fatigue) or perceived (e.g., time restraints, discomfort, anxiety), they are always controllable and, thus, changeable. For instance, the emotional barrier of anxiety (i.e., worry) can be controlled by addressing the source(s) of concern and developing adaptation strategies that overcome these thoughts. A person who is uncomfortable and self-conscious about exercising among younger, fitter, thinner individuals at a fitness facility can focus on his or her exercise regimen, while ignoring others in the room. A person who has time restraints can develop time management strategies and social support by significant others to allow for exercise time.

The importance of performance barriers in the DVM is their root cause—negative habits. These behavioral tendencies, or habits, are labeled "negative" because: (a) the person generally acknowledges that they have a deleterious effect on quality of life, or some aspect of it, and (b) that continued expression of the negative habits is directly linked to problems and limitations in one's personal or professional life. For example, the negative physical habit, "lack of exercise," will lead to low energy and fatigue. The emotional negative habit of persistent anxiety will lead to the negative habit of poor (slow, inaccurate) decision-making or an unpleasant mood. The negative physical habit of poor work/life balance results in poor relationships with family. One function of the model, then, is to help clients detect their negative habits and how they lead to undesirable performance in various aspects of their life, not only health. The primary goal at this stage is that, after negative habits have been associated with performance limitations, the process begins in self-examining the reasons, or "benefits," of maintaining these negative habits, in this case, lack of exercise.

Perceived Benefits of Negative Habits

There are benefits to every negative habit we have. How do we know? Because if there were no benefits, we would not continue to have these negative habits. Think about it. The *benefits* of not exercising include more time to do other things, not experiencing the discomfort of physical exertion, and having expenses related to purchasing fitness club memberships and exercise clothing.

Costs and Long-term Consequences of Negative Habits

Long-term consequences of not exercising include reduced fitness, weight gain, and higher stress and anxiety (both of which are reduced due to exercise). Even longer-term consequences include poorer physical and mental health, reduced quality of life, and, in some cases, shorter lifespan. Are these costs acceptable to the client? If they are, then the negative habit of not exercising and maintaining a sedentary lifestyle will likely continue. However, if the costs are far greater than the benefits, *and* the person concludes that these costs unacceptable, than a change in behavior is far more likely. The process of behavior change is not complete, yet. Missing is the "ignition point," linking the costs of inactivity to the person's deepest values and beliefs.

Determining One's Deepest Values and Beliefs

If you were to give individuals a list of values and then ask them to rank these values according to what is most important to them, they would probably rank health and family near the top. Perhaps integrity, happiness, honesty, character, excellence, commitment, and concern for others would be other highly rated choices.

In order to feel compelled about the long-term commitment and sense of responsibility to exercise, it is important to examine the person's deepest values and beliefs—what he or she finds *really* important. If good health and family are important values, then the person should behave in a way that is consistent with these values and do everything they can to remain an active, healthy family member. After all, others (e.g., children, partners) are depending on them to "be there." Most parents want to see their children mature, graduate, and perhaps marry. This is less likely to be experienced if they do not look after their health. In another example, if the person values integrity, then where is the integrity of placing health and family relatively high in the ranking, yet not demonstrating healthy habits that are consistent with that value? In summary, the decision to begin and maintain an exercise program is more likely if: (a) a person acknowledges that the costs and long-term conse-quences of a negative habit are greater than the benefits, (b) that these costs run counter to the person's deepest values and beliefs about what is important, and finally, (c) that this discrepancy be-tween their negative habits and their values is unacceptable. Thus, behavior change is more likely to be permanent when the patient concludes that life satisfaction is linked to behaving in a way that is consistent with one's deepest values.

Establishing a "Disconnect"

Counseling psychologists might ask clients who do not exercise personal questions such as to what extent are your values consistent with your actions? If you value your health, for instance, do you have habits that are not good for you, and therefore, inconsistent with your values? What about your family? Do you value your spouse, children, or parents? If you lead a sedentary lifestyle and are not involved in a program of exercise, yet one of your deepest values is to maintain good health, to what extent is your value inconsistent with your behavior? Is there a disconnect between your beliefs about good health and your unhealthy behavioral patterns?

Acceptability of the Disconnect

If a person acknowledges that the negative habit of not engaging in exercise is inconsistent with their deepest values and beliefs about what is really important to them, the follow-up question must be to ascertain if this is acceptable. Is the disconnect between these negative habits, such as lack of exercise, and the person's values acceptable? Is it okay, especially after knowing the costs and long-term consequences of this negative habit? If the disconnect *is* accept-able—and for many individuals who feel that changing the negative habit is either undesirable or beyond their control—then no change will likely occur. It is necessary, therefore, to identify another discon-nect between the person's negative habit and their values. Only when the disconnect is unacceptable to the individual is the person prepared to commit to behavior change, and then engage in devel-oping and carrying out an action plan.

Developing a Self-Regulation Action Plan

Developing a self-regulation action plan follows the disconnect between the person's negative habit of nonexercise and their deepest values and beliefs. The plan consists of determining the details of developing a habit of regular exercise during the week. Specifics include type of exercise, exercise location(s), days of the week and times of day exercise will occur, exercise testing to establish a baseline of fitness and health indicators, and availability of social support such as exercising with others and personal fitness coaching, both of which is encouraged. The results of past studies indicate that specificity of timing and precision of behavior dramatically increases the probability of successfully carrying out a self-controlled action plan. The action plan is not unlike a professional golfer who engages in a set of between-shot and pre-shot routines (Bull, Albinson, & Shambrook, 1996).

The action plan consists primarily of three factors that will markedly enhance the individual's *permanent* commitment to regular exercise: (a) a specific time within a 24-hour period for exercise engagement; (b) a set of routines that support the exercise habit (e.g., selected thoughts and behaviors prior to, during, and following the exercise session, exercising with a friend and promoting other forms of social support, minimizing distractions that will interfere with exercise plans), and (c) linking these specific times and routines to the individual's deepest values and beliefs about what is really important, and removing the existing disconnect.

Measuring the Model's Efficacy

How can the MHP measure the model's effectiveness for a client? Examples might include changes in targeted negative habits and in the performance barriers they create, improved attitudes toward exercise, changes in (self-reported) energy level that result from exercise initiation and maintenance, and improved long-term (chronic) positive affect and reduced negative affect/mood. In addition, exercise adherence, intrinsic motivation, and fitness level will each be improved based on self-monitoring (see Appendix A) and record keeping of the individual's exercise habits (see Appendix D). Examples of self-monitoring data include exercise frequency, duration, intensity (identified by heart rate), and content each week, and changes in selected fitness measures (e.g., strength, cardiovascular fitness, percent body fat).

Other measures of the client's change in exercise behavior based on using the model include bi-annual blood testing to detect change in cholesterol and triglycerides, and exercise nonadherence as defined by discontinued physical activity or changes in fitness club or program attendance. Schlenk, Burke, and Rand (2001) point out various measures of adherence/compliance (e.g., erratic noncompliance, unwitting noncompliance, intentional noncompliance). The importance of separating types of nonadherence is to prevent the *abstinence violation effect*, when a single lapse leads the individual to give up on their fitness goals, feel hopeless about attempting to change exercise behavior, and quit exercising (Lox et al., 2003).

Finally, the current model meets the six criteria of a practical and applicable theory or model, as proposed by Brawley (1993):

1. That processes being studied are changeable;

2. That the links between key factors are described so that they are targeted for change;

3. That assessment measures of these factors and the relationships between them are accurate;

4. That the theory or model shows external validity (i.e., it is valid in "real world" settings);

5. That the model's concepts lead to a direct or indirect change in cognition and behavior; and

6. A framework can explain the reasons an intervention failed to produce change.

In summary, critics of existing theories and models in exercise psychology (e.g., Brawley, 1993; Buckworth & Dishman, 2002) and reviewers of the health behavior intervention research (e.g., Glasgow et al., 2004; Marcus & Forsyth, 2003; Nicassio, Meyerowitz, & Kerns, 2004) have been concerned about the paucity of efficacious studies that are based on these theories and models. Establishing long-term exercise habits among sedentary individuals has proven to be very challenging to researchers, clinicians, and practitioners. One limitation in this area has been the absence of a model that captures the individual's self-generated declaration for behavior change.

As Glasgow and colleagues (2004) have concluded about the future of health behavior change research, "If we are serious about evidence-based behavioral medicine and about closing the gap between research findings and application of these findings in applied settings, we cannot continue 'business as usual' " (p. 11). Nicassio and colleagues (2004) suggest that future studies include "specific methodologies for selecting intervention approaches in individual clinical cases" and acknowledging "the mechanisms of action through which interventions achieve their effects" (p. 135). The DVM addresses these concerns in providing a new, innovative approach in examining the antecedents and clinical issues that affect health behavior change. The DVM offers one strategic approach to address possible ways to change behavior and prevent what is becoming a dangerous health crisis in the U.S. and elsewhere.

Chapter 11

Cognitive and Behavioral Strategies to Promote Exercise Performance

Starting and maintaining an exercise program does not happen automatically. Conscious planning of location, time, and performance content is needed, collectively called an *intervention*. Interventions include one or more strategies, categorized as cognitive or behavioral, that are intended to change some predetermined outcome. The purpose of this section is to review the effectiveness of existing interventions; a perusal of the existing research will reveal mixed results. The reasons for these equivocal outcomes will be discussed. New directions in intervention content and effectiveness to change exercise behavior will be suggested.

The primary goal of an intervention is to encourage sedentary or irregularly active individuals to adopt regular exercise habits and to keep physically active persons exercising on a regular basis (Buckworth & Dishman, 2002). Interventions guide what needs to be changed and which strategies should be used.

WHAT MAKES AN INTERVENTION EFFECTIVE?

There have been numerous studies that have tested the effectiveness of specific cognitive or behavioral strategies and interventions on exercise participation and adherence. For example, in their review of this literature, Lox et al. (2003) have identified numerous effective strategies, such as cues-to-action (i.e., stimuli in the environment that prompt exercise participation), self-monitoring (keeping records of progress, including ratings of perceived and activity logs), goal setting, music, personalized performance coaching (also called personal training), social (group) support, and offering positive instructional feedback to improve self-efficacy and develop exercise skills.

Buckworth and Dishman (2002) list four important factors when determining the type of intervention that will lead to adopting and maintaining exercise behavior.

1. *What is the goal?* Changing a person's habit of physical activity is unlike changing other types of health behaviors. The goal here is to adopt and maintain a positive health behavior. The goal is not intended to have the person give up a negative behavior such as smoking cigarettes or overeating.

2. *Exercise is uniquely biologically based.* The effects of exercise, on *biological* outcomes, can be affected by *cognitive* processes such as poor skills, helplessness, or low confidence. The longer-term result could impede intrinsic motivation and exercise enjoyment. Conversely, optimism, confidence, self-control, and concentration will enhance exercise performance and outcome.

3. *Physical activity is a complicated behavior.* There are numerous antecedents and consequences to planning and carrying out an exercise session, including personal issues (e.g., time, location, confidence, self-motivation, energy), social factors (e.g., exercising alone or with a friend, personal comfort at the exercise venue, presence of a personal trainer or other exercise leader), and environmental factors (e.g., location of the exercise session, attraction of the exercise environment, type of equipment). To become a consistent, self-regulated behavior, exercise must be a planned ritual.

4. *Exercise is a dynamic behavior.* Different factors influence exercise adoption, early adherence, long-term adoption, and resumption of exercise after a period of inactivity (called relapse). There is a phenomenon in the exercise psychology literature

called the *abstinence violation effect* (discussed earlier) in which a single lapse in exercise leads an individual to believe that all hope of behavior changes is lost (Lox et al., 2003). The result is a full relapse; permanently quitting future exercise behavior. The type of exercise regimen should match the objectives of an exercise program (e.g., weight loss versus cardiovascular fitness vs. muscular and strength development).

In the following section, we examine the types of strategies that comprise exercise interventions. They are divided into behavioral—reflecting a person's actions—and cognitive—what the person thinks.

Behavioral Strategies

This section will reflect environmental and behavioral factors that encourage continued exercise participation based on the recommendations of several references (e.g., Anshel et al., 2003; Leith, 1998; Sallis & Owen, 1999).

Physical Location

Numerous studies have shown that a person is far more likely to exercise—and adhere to his or her exercise habit—if the exercise facility is located within 3 miles of their home or work. Clients should try to find a location that is either close to where you spend a part of your day or is located on the way to or from work. Should you exercise at home? Since we associate home with relaxation and recovery, rather than with hard physical effort, it is not surprising that people tend to purchase, then stop using, exercise equipment in the home. It is preferred that exercise be performed in an atmosphere that provides incentive by experiencing a "high energy" environment (e.g., bright lights and colors, personal interactions with other exercisers and staff).

Scheduling

We are creatures of routines, not unlike the animal world, to get us through the day. There is a far greater likelihood of exercising if it is planned in advance. The more specific that plan, the better chance it will happen. Choose the time of day that an exercise session is most available and when it feels best—physically and emotionally—to do. However, it is best not to exercise aerobically within 2 hours of bedtime because it reduces time spent in deep (dream) sleep (National Sleep Foundation, 2002).

Introductory Consulting Issues

For the novice, in particular, exercise creates both stress and anxiety. The individual brings to a new program thoughts of previous exercise attempts, fears about experiencing injury or fatigue, and how the body will respond to new exercise demands. There may be worry about his or her appearance and fitness level—fitting in—in a facility that usually attracts younger, fitter individuals. There is often heightened self-consciousness and concerns about performing the exercises correctly and knowledge about proper use of the exercise equipment. But most important of all is the set of personal dispositions that each of us brings to new, challenging situations, especially when performed in the presence of strangers (i.e., other fitness club members).

Novice exercisers need to be welcomed, comforted, and informed. Fitness club staff should determine their members' concerns and how the staff could successfully address them, establish a program of teaching proper exercise techniques, help members set realistic goals, and to help them feel secure in an environment filled with uncertainties, intimidation, and physical and emotional challenges. How can we help people feel comfortable with their present state of fitness and their current physical characteristics that do not match other participants who may be younger and fitter? Exercisers need a sense of belonging to the club, to establish relationships with the people they trust, starting with staff, and to feel secure. The failure to connect with people personally will almost certainly lead to nonattendance.

Goal Setting

Guidelines for setting goals are particularly relevant for the exercise novice. One primary reason for dropping out is the failure to meet goals and expectations, particularly within the first 6 months of starting an exercise program. This is why it is so important to help individuals have realistic expectations about exercise outcomes, and to understand the need to be patient in overcoming years of leading a sedentary lifestyle. The guidelines of having short-term, performance-based goals that are not too challenging will more likely lift confidence and encourage exercise adherence to their program than a person who concludes that they are incapable of meeting excessive demands of the exercise program. Dropping out is preceded by thoughts of helplessness and low self-control.

Sample goals in exercise settings include, "I will complete 20 minutes nonstop on the treadmill," "I will complete three sets of my upper body resistance routine," or "I will reach my training heart rate during interval training." Notice that these goals are *performance* (process) goals, rather than *outcome* (product) goals (e.g., "I will lose 3 pounds" or "I will decrease 2% body fat"), which are long-term, not short-term goals and are under less self-control.

Social Contacts and Interactions

While some exercisers are quite happy to be left alone and to exercise in isolation, most novice performers need to feel connected to others during their routines, a process called *social support* (discussed earlier). The need for social support is especially important in instances when the individual is self-conscious about physical features, and lacks confidence and knowledge about carrying out the exercise routine. Among the first goals of staff should be to introduce themselves to the participant, to instruct participants on exercise equipment, and to develop an exercise protocol. Introducing them to other exercisers is also helpful, especially when the program consists of exercising in a group. If the person exercises at home, his or her family or friends should clearly express support for their exercise habit. Several studies have shown that social support significantly improves exercise adherence.

Rewards

According to positive social reinforcement theory, rewards should have information value about competence. A reward, for example, a t-shirt that reflects achieving a certain level of competence (e.g., 500-mile club) or membership with a group (e.g., the YMCA Running Club) enhances a sense of accomplishment and group member identification. Both outcomes markedly improve participation satisfaction and adherence. In order to build intrinsic motivation, it is best if the reward be linked directly to a desirable performance outcome or achievement, rather than as a response to participation perceived as automatic and expected. The latter loses its value as a reinforcement of competence.

Educational Materials

The written word is a powerful tool in helping people to understand the value of what they do, in this case, exercise. While it is best to avoid complicated research journal articles in providing information to the public, other sources such as magazine articles, book extracts, and materials that reflect credible sources of information and are created by staff provide exercisers with a deeper understanding and justification for their exercise habits. Monthly newsletters with featured articles that address different types of exercises, techniques, and findings from recent studies all have great motivational value.

Clubs, Organizations, and Programs

Humans have a deep need to belong to a group or attend programs in which groups and friendships flourish. They provide comfort, security, and meet social needs. The greater extent to which individuals feel emotionally attached to an exercise program or facility, the more likely they are to return and maintain their involvement. Clubs, weekly lecture and reading groups, banquets that recognize exercise achievement, exercise-related events (e.g., Sunday morning jog), company or individual-sponsored contests (e.g., "The John Smith Annual Run"), outdoor activity club, an annual guest speaker's event, a health-related conference, weekly seminars, and exhibitions by skilled exercisers (e.g., power lifting, aerobic dance) are sample activities that create excitement and motivation to exercise.

Personal Trainer/Instructional Opportunities

This growing area of service in the fitness industry is a welcome addition to facilitating exercise participation. While fitness clubs tend to supply instructors to provide basic instruction and answer member questions, most individuals require more extensive, consistent training. The personal trainer meets this need. High quality trainers have full mastery of fitness science, exercise technique, and nutrition, they know how to help each individual set and achieve personal goals, and they possess the ability to show compassion and genuine interest in their clients. While clients are exercising, trainers should be located near their clients and should be focused on their client's technique. They should assist their clients to keep fitness-related records and even phone them when they have been absent from the facility after a week. The absence of proper exercise technique leads to injury and discomfort resulting in reduced motivation and quitting further exercise.

Environmental Features

Exercise facilities can create an environment that is exciting, intimate and motivating for participants. MHPs can give clients guidance in choosing a fitness facility. In addition to the usual colorful walls and pleasant and upbeat music, management must ensure that their equipment is clean and functions properly. Broken equipment communicates a sense of insensitivity ("we don't care about you"), poor management ("we are not in touch with program needs"), and reduces credibility by not taking the necessary steps to provide high quality equipment to promote fitness. Carpets, workout areas, showers, jacuzzis, swimming pools, locker rooms, and all floors should be clean. There should be separate facilities for confidential meetings with members (e.g., discuss personal information about a member's health or feelings, membership information, personal training instruction). In addition, important information should be easily accessible at the front counter, such as reprints on fitness-related articles and other educational materials, business cards of staff (including the club's manager), and club information (e.g., hours of operation, membership costs). But most important is the atmosphere that staff create by their friendliness, sincerity in helping others, and professional conduct.

Proper Equipment

It is important that the facility have equipment available that meets the needs of all members. Resistance training requires different weight machines for the novice as well as for the advanced power lifter. There are many types of equipment for aerobic training, and as many of these as possible should be made available, and in good working order.

Professional Consulting

Should an MHP be available at a fitness club? This is a novel idea, but given the overweight epidemic, terrible physical condition of most communities, and the large dropout rate at most facilities, perhaps this is an idea whose time has come. What would be the MHP's role and responsibility? What issues would be addressed? How could exercise participants gain access to the person? What would be the costs of this service? Can confidentiality be guaranteed, especially if the service is offered on site in the presence of others? Where would this service be provided? In the facility? Close to a separate entrance to the club? At the MHP's private office away from the facility? And perhaps most important, how would this person function differently than physical training staff? While it is clear clinical services is sometimes needed to address an individual's needs in order to feel more comfortable in an exercise program, less certain is if this service should be provided on site, that is, at an exercise facility.

However, if the provider's title and focus of this service was changed to "Mental Skills Coach" or "Performance Consultant," and the professional dealt with performance-related topics rather than psychotherapy, would this not be more attractive to potential clients? And what if this person worked in coordination with personal trainers, who would work jointly with the clients and refer clients to each other? This could change the whole perception of this type of service. This idea is similar to the concept of "sport psychology consultant" adopted by the Association for the Advancement of Applied Sport Psychology (AAASP).

AAASP has their own certification procedures and certified consultants, and do not refer to themselves as sport psychologists or any other type of psychologist, a title that is reserved for individuals who meet the criteria for licensure in their state. Performance-related issues typically addressed with clients in a fitness club could include: (a) building confidence, (b) managing anxiety related to their exercise participation, (c) teaching clients how to use exercise as a means of stress reduction, (d) providing intervention information to improve client motivation and adherence, (e) helping clients set and achieve goals, (f) teaching the proper use of mental skills that enhance exercise performance (psyching up, imagery, etc.), (g) providing social support, (h) linking the strengths of each personal trainer with the unique needs of each client, and (i) being the liaison for participants who need to communicate with club staff, with management, or someone to whom they can turn for advice.

Record Keeping

The importance of having exercisers keep records gets at the heart of intrinsic motivation—perceived competence. It is important that exercise leaders and physical trainers work with clients to record baseline measures of various dimensions of fitness, then monitor progress through maintaining those records. In this way, exercisers can detect indicators of improvement and achievement, which are important sources of intrinsic motivation in which the person's drive to participate in an activity reflects satisfaction, enjoyment, and a sense of achievement. Performance data should be recorded, updated, and monitored in quantitative form, reflecting numbers, rather than general comments, such as "Susan did a good job today" or "Sid is feeling better about is exercise progress." Examples should include time—minutes and seconds—of aerobic activity, the amount of resistance lifted, the number of repetitions, degrees of flexibility (stretching), changes in percent body fat, number of laps or distance jogged, and even frequency of attending the fitness venue or a particular program. Sarafino (1994) contends "seeing on paper how far they have progressed can be very reinforcing" (p. 267).

Exerciser Checklist/Self-Monitoring

Developing an exercise habit requires learning a vast array of new skills and initiating many new routines to ensure a successful and pleasant experience. As indicated earlier, starting a new exercise program is intimidating and stressful–both mentally and physically. Perhaps it is not surprising that so many people quit exercise programs, given the amount of energy expended in finding the time to exercise, preparing for and engaging in the actual exercise activity, and then dealing with the physical challenges of overcoming a sedentary lifestyle. The novice exerciser needs help—and plenty of it. This is the value of an exerciser checklist, which I have developed while working with exercisers for many years.

The technique, called *self-monitoring* in the psychology literature, entails listing the thoughts, emotions, and actions that should be part of the exerciser's weekly and daily protocol. There are no "right" or "wrong" answers. This is not a "test" of knowledge, but rather, a set of guidelines about making exercise as pleasant and performed as efficiently as possible. Thus, answers as close to "5" as possible are always desirable. Items that are answered 1 through 3 require attention about the source(s) of this low score. The goal in completing this checklist is to improve (increase) the total score for each segment.

The checklist should be reviewed by the exerciser's personal trainer or performance consultant—for novices, once per week, probably less often after the first month. After 4 to 6 weeks of consistent monitoring, the checklist serves as an occasional reminder of things to do, but is less important in fostering exercise adherence than at earlier stages of developing exercise routines. Finally, selected items on the checklist may be irrelevant to some individuals. For example, an exerciser may prefer to exercise alone rather than exercising with others. Therefore, the item that addresses exercising in a group setting can be eliminated from the checklist. The Exerciser Checklist is located in Appendix A.

Provide Feedback on Performance

Providing information to exercisers, particularly about their level of competence and improvement, raises their level of confidence and enhances intrinsic motivation. Information that is critical, yet constructive, also has this effect, because constructive criticism serves the purposes of improving skills, knowledge, and performance outcomes. Anshel (2003b) provides key guidelines for performance feedback and other communication techniques. Briefly, however, all information feedback—in both positive and critical forms—should reflect observable and measurable behavior (e.g., "great effort on staying on task"), rather than reflect more abstract content (e.g., "you're looking better" or "nice going."). Giving feedback *intermittently* is more effective than giving it constantly. The important issue here is that exercisers need to hear and observe positive messages about their performance or about outcomes derived from their efforts.

Monitor Client Attendance

It is important to keep tabs on who is present and who is absent from the exercise venue. Absences provide the first warning sign of quitting. While it is possible that individuals are deciding to exercise in locations other than formal programs and clubs, a person's commitment to an ongoing program of physical activity is strongly tied to developing relationships with individuals at the exercise venue. If clients have not attended the venue in a week, they should be contacted to determine the reason for their absence. This strategy will markedly improve adherence.

Use Small, Attainable Units to Reflect Progress

As indicated earlier, building intrinsic motivation to perform any task is strongly linked to building perceptions of competence. This is best accomplished when the exercise detects increments of improvement, however small. The exercise program, then, should contain measures that are somewhat easy to attain and that reinforce the performer's perception of moving toward achieving their goals. This is why using the relatively small unit of time (minutes, for example) is more likely to reflect competent performance than measuring performance by the relatively larger unit of distance (miles, for instance).

Social Support

As discussed earlier, the likelihood to adhere to an exercise program increases significantly if a friend or family member accompanies the exerciser, or if the exerciser receives emotional support (e.g., praise, recognition, approval) for their efforts or on the positive outcomes from their exercise participation. Nonverbal social support comes with providing ways to facilitate the exerciser's habit, such as driving a person to the exercise venue, giving a fitness club membership as a gift, or supervising or monitoring the exerciser's responsibilities (e.g., babysitting, performing work-related tasks, recording a favorite T.V. program). As Sarafino (1994) contends, "people are more likely to start and stick with an exercise program if these efforts have the support and encouragement of family and friends" (p. 267).

Perceived Choice

It makes no sense to force a person to engage in a certain type of exercise, or to use a certain piece of equipment if they have negative feelings about it. For example, overweight individuals will often dislike treadmills. This is understandable, since a treadmill forces the person to perform aerobically, while attempting to overcome additional sources of discomfort (e.g., bodyweight, sore knees, bad back). The best approach would be to give exercisers choices about the types of activities they can perform that will have similar health and fitness benefits. At first, the novice should develop proper technique before they attempt to be challenged physically. Tasks should be kept relatively easy at first, then slowly increased in task difficulty.

Social Engineering

Think of what we can do—how we can physically change our environment—to reduce external demands on us? Driving down a less-traveled road, going to a restaurant at a less-crowded time, or attending a fitness facility at a less-busy time. The concept of social engineering comes from the stress management literature, in which persons will experience less stress if locating themselves in a place in which fewer environmental sources of stress are present. If possible, the novice should exercise at a time when equipment is more likely to be available and when the staff can offer more attention and instruction. Even more important for the highly self-conscious exerciser is that fewer people in attendance means less likelihood of being observed by others, at least that may be the exerciser's perception.

Music

It is well known, according to scientific studies (e.g., Anshel & Marisi, 1978) and from empirical observations, that more intense music has an arousal-inducing effect on exercise performance. Exercise facilities acknowledge this and often have music playing throughout their facility. Some exercisers prefer their music and wear headsets or Walkmans. Music has the advantage of distracting the exerciser from boredom and the physical manifestations of vigorous physical activity (e.g., fatigue, sweating, extreme effort). Music also improves the exerciser's mood state. However, music can also reduce concentration on the task at hand, resulting in lower performance quality. It's all a matter of personal preference and monitoring.

Modeling

Rather than feeling intimidated by highly fit exercisers, one source of motivation is to observe the high-level performance of another exerciser. The long-term goal, here, is to observe their exercise techniques and to use their high performance quality as a source of inspiration and motivation to pursue fitness and health-related goals. As your fitness improves you will begin to perform at a similar level.

Time of Day

Not surprisingly, each of us differs on the time of day we prefer to exercise. This is due to both personal choice—feeling more like exercising at a certain time—and due to the time that is available to us. Does time of day make a difference in how the body responds to exercise and to exercise outcomes? Not according to a study by O'Connor and Davis (1992), who confirmed the findings of several earlier Swedish studies. While the benefits are similar no matter what time one exercises, it is best not to exercise aerobically within 3 hours of going to sleep. Studies also indicate that high intensity aerobic exercise close to bedtime will reduce time spent in deep sleep.

Lifestyle Management

The effects of exercising and improved fitness are not experienced in a vacuum. The goals of weight control, fat reduction, gains in strength, firmness, and cardiovascular fitness must be accompanied by other healthy habits, such as proper nutrition and diet, sufficient sleep, and maintaining work/life balance. The workaholic who exercises vigorously, yet neglects other important behaviors and ignores his or her family and friends is often lacking personal happiness, remains highly stressed, and is likely to succumb to sickness or disease. Exercise becomes just one more thing to have to do, rather than as a form of recovery and enjoyment. Fitness should be one segment, albeit an important one, of an overall lifestyle that creates a source of joy and life satisfaction.

Cognitive Strategies

This section concerns the use of mental skills that favorably influence exercise performance. Most of these have been established in the sport psychology literature and used successfully in sport settings, and they also have a direct impact on exercise performance.

Visualization/Imagery

Visualization, also referred to interchangeably as imagery, consists of thoughts that form mental representations of physical performance. While the use of visualization, or mental imagery, is a common and effective technique in improving sports performance, the exerciser can also use this strategy to gain confidence, learn new exercise routines, reduce tension and anxiety prior to exercising, increase excitation and psychological readiness, and improve motivation. The exerciser should find time and a location that is void of visual or auditory distractions, and then take a few minutes to relax; relaxation causes the image to become more vivid and realistic. Then, think through the environmental features, specific exercises, and sensations and feelings experienced during the exercise routine in a highly desirable, positive manner. Mentally rehearse the activity, as performed in *perfect* form, and followed by a desirable outcome.

Bizarre Imagery

While normal imagery is a mental representation of *real life situations*, bizarre imagery is a mental representation of *nonrealistic events*. For example, cancer patients are sometimes asked to imagine their tumors being shrunk as they receive chemotherapy. Cardiac or pulmonary patients might imagine rapid changes in their circulatory system that are medically impossible during an exercise bout. An overweight person might imagine fat being "dissolved" or arteries being "widened" while exercising. The purpose of bizarre imagery is to heighten exercise motivation and to distract the person from the challenges presented from the exercise task.

Association/Dissociation

During physical exertion, should you focus your attention on the muscles being used or to ignore bodily sensations and become distracted from the task at hand? Conscious attempts at linking the mind and body is called *association*. An example of properly using association is during strength training. The focus of attention should be on the muscle group being used to lift the weight. *Dissociation*, on the other hand, is used when the exerciser wants to ignore bodily responses. Examples include distance running, or someone undergoing exercise rehabilitation whose therapy requires movements that are uncomfortable.

Thought-Stopping

A common dilemma in exercise is engaging in self-statements that reveal unpleasant feelings about the task at hand. Unpleasant feelings, especially if continued during an exercise bout, may lead to demotivation, reduced effort, and even dropping out from further participation. The suggestion here is that in response to negative feelings, exercisers should say to themselves "STOP!" The effect is that the negative thoughts will go away. This is because the command to "stop" will remind the exerciser of the unpleasant effects of the negative, self-induced messages and allow the person to regain their proper mental set to a more positive, uplifting message. Thoughts go from irrational to rational.

Positive Self-Talk

Instead of negative self-talk (e.g., "This is terrible," "I feel awful," or "I can hardly wait until this is over"), the exerciser wants to engage in a more uplifting, motivating message. The result will be more effort and intensity, better concentration, and greater enjoyment of the task. Examples in exercise settings include, "Let's do it," "I feel good," and "Stay with it." The use of single words that influence mood are also effective, such as "Go," "Focus," and "Get it!"

Anticipation

The ability to predict a movement before performing it increases momentum, improves pre-performance readiness, and reduces the amount of information the person must process quickly. This strategy is especially important when performing fast-paced, coordinated activity, common in aerobic workouts.

Psyching Up

For some activities, in which high arousal and energy are required (e.g., physical exercise), the performer's thought processes must be upbeat and "active." A cognitive technique called *psyching up* consists of thinking about the task at hand and having thoughts of excitation, challenge, spirited, engaged, connected, and high energy. The goal of psyching up is to improve arousal level usually accompanied by increased physiological responses. Psyching up can be experienced in either physical or mental form. Physically, the person can engage in tasks that require increased energy and heightened somatic responses (e.g., higher heart rate, respiration rate, muscle tension). Mentally, psyching up usually consists of thoughts that increase confidence, motivation, and concentration. Examples of psyching up types of thoughts include "let's do it," "focus," and "I'm ready." Whereas positive self-talk improves confidence and concentration, and *regulates* intensity level, psyching up is strictly intended to *increase* cognitive and physiological forms of arousal. This strategy should be used only in tasks and situations in which high energy is desirable.

Location Cues

This mental skill is more for exercises that have predetermined starting and ending points, such as stretching, weight training, and yoga. It can also be used for certain aerobic activities that consist of specific steps and motions, such as foot or hand placements, in completing the move. A sample location cue would be to tell a person to have a 45 degree angle at the elbow before performing a lift, or planting one's foot "at 2 o'clock," indicating the angle at which the foot should be placed or point when hitting the floor. Tennis players, for instance, are asked to strike the ball "at 2 o'clock," using the clock face as a model.

Attribution Training

This strategy (reviewed extensively in chapter 4 of Anshel, 2003b) has strong implications in exercise settings. An exerciser, particularly a novice, will be physically challenged to complete one or more exercises despite a significant increase in effort, sweating, and fatigue. Exercisers should interpret their attempts as successful, and then attribute this success to high effort. Linking effort to success has very high motivation value and feelings of competence and self-control. Even experiencing fatigue and not meeting performance expectations can be attributed to task difficulty, and sometimes to low effort—if this is an accurate cause. Low performance quality should rarely be attributed to low ability. On the other hand, a few individuals who find it very difficult to move in a coordinated manner during an aerobics class might accurately conclude that a poor sense of coordination is responsible for less than desirable performance.

Building Intrinsic Motivation (IM)

While building IM is not, in itself, a cognitive strategy, it is a necessary component of a long-term commitment to exercise. For promoting exercise, it is important that the two main components, self-determination (high self-control) and information (high perceived competence) be addressed. Thus, the exerciser should make his or her own decision about the need to exercise, choose what type of exercise program and where the program should be located, feel confident about their ability to engage in exercise, and finally, receive positive feedback about their exercise success and competence.

Examining Personal Values and Beliefs

This area was covered in more depth in Chapter 10, but warrants a brief overview here as a strategy to enhance a person's commitment to exercise. According to Dr. Jack Groppel (2000), in order to feel compelled about the long-term commitment and sense of responsibility to exercise, it is important to examine the person's deepest values and beliefs—what is really important to him or her. If good health and family are important values, then the person should behave in a way that is consistent with these values. They want to live a long time, because their family is depending on them. In addition, no doubt the person would like to live and remain healthy in order to see his or her children grow up and to enjoy retirement. If the person values integrity, then they should be keeping promises and be true to their standards and ideals. The person should be reminded of the cost-benefit tradeoff, that is, the benefits versus the costs of not exercising. Are these costs acceptable? If they run counter to the individual's deepest values and beliefs, hopefully not.

INTERVENTION IMPLICATIONS FROM PREVIOUS THEORIES AND MODELS

The extant theories and models in the health psychology literature, described in chapter 3, explain the factors that best predict health behaviors. Their effectiveness in changing exercise behavior, however, is questionable. Taken together, the amount of outcome variance explained in studies testing the efficacy of exercise interventions has rarely been above 30% (Baranowski, Anderson, & Carmack, 1998). Prior to examining a new model that fosters exercise behaviors, it is important to examine the implications of this literature for exercise participation and adherence.

Theory of Reasoned Action and Theory of Planned Behavior

Implications for applying concepts from Theory of Reasoned Action (TRA) and Theory of Planned Behavior (TPB) include developing social support, perhaps exercising with a friend, receiving positive feedback about their exercise habits (e.g., "it's great that you are exercising"), and providing information about the desirable outcomes from regular exercise participation (e.g., "you are looking great"). A social component of the exercise program, perhaps by developing friendships at their fitness club or exercising with a friend, is also valuable. In addition, the exerciser should be in control of all decisions surrounding the exercise program, including the time (days of the week and time of day), location, duration, and program content. This is where a commitment to working with a physical trainer would be helpful, at least during the initial stages of an exercise program.

The Health Belief Model

According to the Health Belief Model (HBM), for example, motivating individuals to exercise includes *providing educational materials* that address the benefits of exercise and the costs of leading a sedentary lifestyle, *modeling proper exercise habits and routines*—this is where hiring a physical trainer and receiving instruction is so valuable, *enhancing the exerciser's perceived competence* (e.g., "I can do this," "I have good technique"), *improving perceived exercise effectiveness* (e.g., "I'm improving;" "My health is improving"), *elevating self-effi-cacy, or confidence* (e.g., "I feel comfortable exercising; it is becoming easier"), *developing set exercise routines* (e.g., "I know exactly when, where, and how I will exercise"), and *establishing easy access to an exercise facility* (preferably within a short distance of work, home, or between these locations). Quitting an exercise habit tends to be far more common when the person relies only on home exercise equipment, since we associate our home environment with relaxation and recreation, not with challenging levels of physical exertion, sweating, and physical fatigue commonly associated with exercise.

The Transtheoretical Model

With respect to the transtheoretical model, Buckworth and Dishman (2002) provide goals and strategies for each of the five stages. For example, at the *precontemplation stage*, the goal is to begin thinking about changing behavior. Strategies include informing individuals about the role of exercise in good health, strengthening the actual and perceived personal benefits of exercise, and reducing perceived costs and other barriers to exercise.

The goal at the *contemplation stage* should be to adopt regular exercise habits. The strategies should be to market accurate, understandable guidelines for exercise novices, provide activities to increase exercise efficacy (e.g., mastery experiences), and evaluate pros and cons of exercise. Persons at the *preparation stage* should adopt regular exercise at the appropriate targeted level. Strategies should include setting reasonable, realistic, but challenging goals, and evaluate and modify barriers, if needed.

The *action state* includes establishing exercise as a habit, and to use behavior modification (i.e., use of reward and reinforcement and self-monitoring) to prevent relapse. Structured exercise sessions (e.g., an aerobics class), positive reinforcement (e.g., praise from significant others), and test data that show improvement on various dimensions (e.g., improved cholesterol measures, reduced percent body fat, improved cardiovascular functioning, strength gains) would be helpful. Finally, the *maintenance stage* should have as its primary goal sustaining lifelong regular exercise. Strategies would include re-evaluating exercise goals, introducing variety into the exercise routine, and planning how to deal effectively with potential sources of relapse.

Improved outcomes from this model would include matching the intervention treatment to the individual's stage of change, progressing one stage at a time (Berger et al., 2002). Thus, a person who is in the contemplation stage needs a personal invitation to work out, preferably by someone with whom he or she feels comfortable, education about the benefits of exercise, and a high degree of structure in preparing for and scheduling their exercise routine.

Two Strategies for Improving Exercise Adherence

The most common reasons for dropping out of an exercise program include not meeting (very high) expectations, lack of enjoyment, injury, and lack of time. Maintaining an exercise program is called *adherence*. You can adhere to an exercise regimen if you follow a few important guidelines.

Have Realistic Expectations

It takes time to become overweight and out of shape. Fortunately, it takes less time to become more fit. This is because muscles were made to move; we need exercise. A sedentary lifestyle means that exercise is a struggle. Don't be impatient about experiencing the benefits of physical activity. Over time, usually within six weeks, exercise will improve your fitness level, physical appearance, self-esteem, and even your mental health. At the same time, your body weight may not decrease dramatically. Do not quit. Be patient.

Do Not Concentrate on Body Weight

Your weight scale is not telling you the truth, especially after you begin an exercise program. It fails to disclose how much of your weight is *fat* and how much of your weight is *muscle*. Since muscle weighs more than fat, and you gain muscle through exercise, your body weight may or may not change. But your fitness has improved dramatically and you are much healthier. The scale, which reflects weight loss, can certainly be a motivator to continue an exercise program. But remember that weight loss is usually not the primary purpose to exercise. Your health should be the main reason. According to a study by Blair and Brodney published in the journal, *Medicine and Science in Sport* (1999), people who are overweight or obese experience similar physical and mental benefits from exercise as individuals of normal weight.

Receive Instruction on Proper Ways to Exercise

Proper exercise technique must be learned. Invest in a personal trainer (not just anyone, but someone who really cares about helping you) and learn to exercise properly. This way, you will exercise more efficiently, with less effort, and you will improve your fitness more quickly. Also, remember to warm up and cool down properly, drink water before and during your exercise session, and stretch *after* your exercise session.

Schedule Your Exercise Times and Places

So many of us feel there is insufficient time to exercise during the day. *Plan your exercise times in advance*; prepare your exercise gear the night before (store it in your car, leave it by the door on your way out, or rent a locker at your gym). Joining a fitness club has its advantages—if you can afford it. Rarely do we feel motivated to exercise at home. This is because we associate home with relaxation and recreation, and rarely with engaging in vigorous physical activity. This is why exercise equipment usually sits unused in so many homes. It might be better to join a fitness club where the atmosphere is motivating to exercise, where you might meet friends, get support for your exercise program, and use high quality equipment.

Social Support

Clients should exercise with a friend, or at least make sure a client's spouse/partner or family supports his or her exercise habits. Several studies have shown that surrounding oneself with others who encourage exercise significantly improves exercise adherence.

Combine Aerobic and Strength Exercises

If your client wants to benefit from exercise, don't forget two areas that need attention, the cardiovascular system (aerobic work) and strength training. Both have enormous benefits to good mental and physical health. Aerobic exercise, in particular, leads to improved self-esteem, reduced anxiety, and heightened tolerance to stress. Stretching exercises improve joint flexibility and help reduce the onset of injury and discomfort.

Feel a Sense of Achievement and Competence From Exercising

Central to internal motivation is a sense of satisfaction, achievement, and competence derived from your exercise program. Use data— numbers, such as changes in exercise time (speed), resistance, repetitions, frequency, distance, and so on—to indicate improved change over time.

Anxiety

Anxiety consists of feelings of worry or threat about the future. "Will I succeed?" "I hope I can lose weight," "What if I look ridiculous in front of all those people?" Sources of exercise anxiety include worry about meeting goals, our physical appearance, being accepted by others (especially strangers), and using time to exercise instead of doing something else ("I could be watching TV or finishing a report instead of going to the gym"). Incredibly, exercise reduces anxiety, both short term (acute anxiety) and long term (chronic anxiety). Exercise is what the doctor ordered for improved *mental* health.

High Self-Expectations

Too many people quit exercise programs when their unrealistic expectations (e.g., losing 20 pounds in a month, being able to keep up with your fitness instructor, eliminating excessive fat from the tummy or thighs) are not met. You want improvement! Results take more time, please be patient.

Low Perceived Competence

We almost never persist at anything about which we feel inadequate. Conversely, we are attracted to and engage in tasks at which we feel competent. Clients should learn the proper exercise techniques and practice them. Hiring a personal trainer is a good investment if the trainer is truly interested in improving fitness.

Negative Self-Talk

It is impossible to remain motivated and "on task" if clients are saying to themselves, "I don't like this," "I feel terrible," or "I'm tired." Turn those thoughts around. Stay optimistic and enthusiastic. Positive self-talk includes "I can do this," "I feel good," "just three more minutes to go," and "hang in there." A person cannot be unhappy and enthusiastic at the same time.

Perfectionism

For some people, it's never good enough. It can always be better. Perfectionist exercisers should eliminate that "little guy on the shoulder" that serves as a reminder that it's "still not good enough." Perfectionists are high achievers, no question. They persist longer on task and improve and achieve more with time and effort than nonperfectionists. So far, so good! However, the down side of being a perfectionist, a condition called neurotic perfectionism, is to set goals that are unachievable and in which the person is almost never feel satisfied. Their expectations of others are also excessive. Be careful. Set reasonable goals and recognize when they are achieved, especially in exercise. Have *indicators* of success. Don't try to look like someone from a magazine cover or movie star. Be you—just try to get better.

Lack of Social Support

Many people cannot do it all alone. Who doesn't need encouragement once in awhile? It's normal to need our friends, spouse, and family to recognize and support us in our exercise habit. Social support can come from exercising with a partner or in a group setting, getting to know others at the fitness club who exercise at the same time, working with a personal trainer, or telling a friend about your exercise habits and progress.

In conclusion, interventions are a useful tool for meeting numerous goals related to exercise participation. These include improving exercise performance, enhancing intrinsic motivation, overcoming the person's individual barriers to begin and maintain a regular exercise regimen, and feeling comfortable in an exercise environment. The challenge for most exercise professionals is to develop ways that create and maintain a strong fitness ethic, and making exercise a way of life for the previously sedentary individual. As Buckworth and Dishman (2002) have concluded, "traditional interventions have not addressed the cyclical or dynamic nature of exercise behavior, and the dropout rate from structured exercise programs has remained at 50% for the past 25 years" (p. 253). They concluded that the best approaches to encouraging the adoption and long-term maintenance of an active lifestyle include "environments that prompt increased activity, offer accessible facilities, remove real and perceived barriers, and reward physical activity" (p. 253). Clearly, additional research is needed to test intervention effectiveness and the optimal environmental conditions and the exerciser's personal characteristics that should accompany each strategy.

Chapter 12

Maintaining Quality Control: Personal Trainers, Fitness Facilities, and Proper Programs

Starting an exercise program, even with the assistance and encouragement of MHPs and other professionals, is not easy. It's important to remember that it takes years to develop habits, including negative habits that are not beneficial to our health and well-being, with which we've become very comfortable. The lifestyle of most Western cultures consisting of an increasingly sedentary lifestyle, lack of exercise, and over-indulgence in food leading to excessive weight gain, has lead to greater deterioration in health. Each year we are getting sicker! There's plenty of blame to go around that helps explain our current health crisis—which, by the way, is getting worse each year as supported by the continued climb in the average weight of all age groups, and increased health costs. The purpose of this chapter is to focus on one source of the problem—the fitness industry—and to help MHPs to provide credible counsel to their clients in selecting proper exercise facilities, programs, and personnel in starting and maintaining an exercise program. Let's have a look at how your clients can select the most credible and effective support system that will make a significant contribution toward developing and maintaining a proper exercise program. In addition to the MHP, other members of the support system include personal trainers, fitness facilities, and choosing the correct programs.

SELECTING AN EXERCISE FACILITY

One important reason I have devoted a chapter to selecting and attending an appropriate, high-quality exercise facility is that it is so difficult to experience a proper exercise workout at home. Have you noticed how often people purchase fitness equipment, only to have it sit idle in the home just days or weeks later? Why is that? Why spend hundreds of dollars, or more, and not use the equipment? The reasons vary, but it is mainly because we perceive our home environment as a place to relax and recover from the turmoil of our jobs and other external pressures. In addition, we become involved in a vast array of activities in and around our homes that distract us from engaging in regular exercise. In other words, we have not ritualized our exercise program. Certainly we do not have the array of equipment at home that exists in a fitness club. Finally, we have no performance coaching, no instruction, and no sources of motivation at home that are often inherent in exercise facilities. No wonder we let our equipment just sit there and collect dust. For these reasons, many individuals find the exercise facility to be a wise investment in time and money if it is used regularly. Here are some guidelines for ensuring that fitness clubs are selected and used properly.

Personal Trainers and Other Staff

Perhaps no other factor lends itself more to effective exercise outcomes than the level of staff quality. As a former member of this industry, I can attest to the wide variety of staff talent and commitment to excellence that can significantly affect the quality of service to participants. Most trainers have superb knowledge in the proper use of weight machines, can provide fitness tests and exercise prescriptions, and genuinely care about their client's welfare and performance. Others, on the other hand, are less interested in these aspects of the job and attend more to their own fitness, financial, and social needs then to their client. The following guidelines serve as important reminders about the need to obtain high-quality coaching as part of your client's exercise experience at a fitness facility.

Staff Qualifications

Today, more than ever, various types of certifications exist that require extensive training and grasp of important concepts that will serve all exercise participants. Organizations such as the American Council of Sports Medicine (ACSM), the American Council on Exercise (ACE), and many others each have certification criteria and standards that qualify an individual to provide exercise leadership and counsel. Appendix B includes a list and contact information of these organizations.

Important Questions

Before a client engages in exercise at the facility, good instructors ask participants about their medical conditions, exercise history, and previous injuries that may affect an exercise experience. For example, determining a person's exercise history will alert the staff person about how much additional knowledge the exerciser requires. If a person has suffered from low back pain or other source of discomfort it is important to provide that individual with "do's and don'ts" about proper and improper movements, especially if the condition was serious. Advice about the proper ways to engage in an exercise class, often misunderstood by novices, will markedly enhance the level of enjoyment and outcome. Current medications ingested by the client forms another important area of inquiry, including a note from the client's physician.

Modeling

Good instructors model all exercises and demonstrate and explain correct body alignment and form. In fact, it is preferred to have pre-exercise instruction for a few minutes before the class. This means that the staff member should look presentable—dressed in proper exercise clothing—and appear fit. Similar to physicians who lose credibility if they are overweight or smoke, fitness instructors should appear as though they follow their own advice.

Exercise Leadership Qualities

Many fitness center staff and personal coaches also lead exercise classes. Without question, these individuals should be certified by a national organization (see Appendix B for a list of these organizations). One characteristic of high-quality instructors is moving around the room during the class to observe members, provide feedback, and assist in improving movement quality. In addition, the instructor will monitor intensity levels throughout the class by teaching clients to determine heart rate by taking their pulse. Another quality of good fitness leaders is being available before and after the class to allow participants to ask questions. Finally, some instructors are more concerned with the quality of their own workout rather than focusing on the participants' workout. Instructors should be friendly and show genuine concern about the quality of each client's workout.

Supporting Staff Quality

Other staff that support the program include individuals who work the desk, sell memberships, cleaners, and managers of the facility. Are they friendly, open to feedback, efficient in their job, and properly attired? The quality of facility management can often be detected by the quality of support staff.

FITNESS FACILITIES

Imagine the degree of intimidation experienced by many individuals who walk into a facility filled with relatively fit, perhaps younger individuals whose physical appearance and skills in performing an array of exercises are far superior to the unfit, overweight, relatively unskilled novice. It is no wonder that the fitness club industry has a membership dropout rate of about 60%; that is, almost two-thirds of individuals who take out a club membership do not renew it. The fact that about 50% of new exercisers quit within 3 to 6 months is also not surprising given the lack of instruction and mentoring from this industry. What's the problem? What is this industry doing wrong that is leading to this extensive dropout rate, and what can they do differently? What should a prospective member look for in a facility before becoming a member? Here are some criteria.

Location

One predictor of exercise participation and adherence is access to an exercise facility. An inconvenient location in which the person must drive one or two miles outside their normal travel route between home and work often leads to exercise dropout. Key questions exercisers should ask before taking out a club membership are:

(a) Is this facility convenient to my home or work?
(b) Will I pass the facility frequently during daily errands?
(c) Is the facility in a location that I feel comfortable driving to and walking to and from my car?

Standards for Fitness Facility

The American College of Sport Medicine (2001) recommends six standards for proper exercise facilities. A facility must:

(a) have an appropriate emergency plan;
(b) offer each adult member fitness pre-activity screening. The Physical Activity Readiness Questionnaire (PAR-Q) is recommended as a minimal standard for a person's entry into a moderate intensity exercise program. The PAR-Q is meant to assist staff in determining if the client is at increased risk or has symptoms for cardiovascular, pulmonary, or metabolic disease, and to optimize safety during exercise programming;
(c) include management staff that demonstrates professional competence (e.g., good communication skills, handling problems or emergencies, responding to member inquiries);
(d) offer childcare services that includes supervision;
(e) conform to all relevant laws, regulations, and published standards for cleanliness, fire exits, building codes, and other aspects of operating the facility; and
(f) maintain a clean facility (e.g., towels and papers are picked up, soap is in dispensers, carpet is vacuumed, exercise machines are cleaned and dusted).

A tour of the facility should reveal the following:

(a) Is the facility large enough to handle the number of people who want to exercise at the peak time of day? Future members should tour the facility during peak hours, which are from 6 to 8 a.m., 12 to 2 p.m., and 5 to 8 p.m.

(b) Does the facility have the type of resistance training and cardio fitness equipment that match the person's goals?

(c) Is the equipment clean and maintained or are several machines in disrepair?

(d) Is there a separate room for aerobic exercise, and is this room large enough to support the number of members in an average class? Does this room include a supportive (flexible) floor, or is it situated on less desirable concrete?

(e) Does the facility have good ventilation, and is it kept at a comfortable temperature for exercise?

(f) Are the classes and programs offered at convenient times that fit the person's anticipated workout schedule?

(g) Does the facility offer the types of classes that match the person's goals and interests?

(h) Are the clientele people I would feel comfortable working out with?

When anticipating club membership, a tour of the facility by staff during the hours the person intends to use the facility is essential, and there should never be hesitation to ask questions.

Fitness Programs

The facility should accommodate an array of programs, one of which would meet the person's needs. Here are some criteria for high-quality programs.

(a) The member should complete a health screening form and be asked questions about the member's current health status, previous health concerns, injuries, medications, and physical conditions that might affect exercise tolerance.

(b) Ideally, selected fitness tests should be administered, although this is usually an extra charge beyond the membership fee. Testing serves two primary functions: to detect any abnormalities that may give rise to concern about the person's exercise tolerance, and to serve as baseline measures from which to compare future exercise performance—a measure of improved fitness.

(c) Personal training should be available. A personal trainer, as previously discussed in this chapter, is a person paid an extra fee who will provide the member instruction on selected types of exercises, test current fitness level, and devise a program that will meet the member's personal fitness goals.

(d) Exercise programs might include various types of cardio classes (e.g., stop, low impact, cycling, rowing, boxing, tae bo), aquatic classes (e.g., water aerobics, swimming), yoga, Pilates, tai chi, resistance training, sports skill instruction, and seminars on health-related topics.

Costs

Membership costs should be closely examined before a person commits to joining the facility. What does the cost include and what services are extra? Personal coaching might include a one-time-only demonstration of selected machines or initial, general advice. However, more meaningful and in-depth coaching will likely cost extra. How much extra requires asking questions. Other pointers:

Does the facility staff review and explain all initial costs, extra costs, payment methods, policies, and cancellation procedures? Does the client feel pressured to join or to commit for a certain length of time, let's say two years for a reduced cost versus one year? Is the client given time to think about this decision? Is there pressure to sign "on the dotted line" before they leave or else membership costs will go higher? Is a free pass recommended before purchasing a full membership? What is the policy for guests? These are questions that warrant open and candid answers. Are the answers clear and candid? Your financial status and your health are dependent on making the right choice, so take your time and do not feel pressure to move quickly on this important decision.

In summary, selecting an exercise facility is a very important investment in one's future health. The MHPs first challenge is to give clients the needed confidence to enter this facility and become comfortable with the surroundings and with staff. It is advised that novice exercisers attend the facility with a friend or partner to help make a wise decision about future membership. It is also a good idea to take advantage of a guest pass that allows free use of the facility for a certain time period, even one time, so that the individuals feels comfortable in the facility and its users. MHPs might want to tour various facilities in the community in which they practice so that they can speak of first hand knowledge about its appearance, services, clientele, cleanliness, and quality of management. Indeed, some MHPs might want to consider approaching exercise club management and offer a service of personalized consulting as part of, or in addition to, the services rendered, an issue addressed in chapter 13.

Chapter 13

Future Directions
in Exercise Consulting

This book serves the primary purpose of providing information and insight into a virtually untapped and underserved area in the profession of mental health consulting—helping clients improve their health and quality of life through exercise. Clinical and counseling psychology programs are laden with courses that address understanding client needs and developing cognitive and behavioral techniques to improve mental health. Yet, the area of exercise as an important strategy to overcome a client's personal "storms" receives no attention in the curriculum. Although informed psychologists often suggest that clients start exercising or join a fitness facility, clients often require emotional support and information to facilitate this process that most MHPs (nor anyone else) are not providing. The result is that clients begin a program, only to drop out within weeks or months. Hopefully, this book will encourage many MHPs to reconsider their role in the process of lending encouragement and support to clients in successfully pursuing an exercise program.

The purpose of this chapter is to discuss future directions in the consulting process and to generate ideas and strategies to move this area forward. Ideally, every MHP would incorporate an exercise component with every client (if possible) in their private practice.

PRIVATE CONSULTING OPPORTUNITIES

The area of applied exercise psychology has explosive potential for private practitioners. While it is true that MHPs cannot be all things to all people, and that each practitioner should determine, develop, and then market his or her expertise, the ability to lend counsel in applied exercise psychology is easily achievable—and needed. There is a public whose collective health is at great risk, and in great need of expertise, guidance, and support in the area of exercise. No one else has better skills of building relationships and trust, while disseminating knowledge that can permanently change the lives of others.

The Corporate Sector

The business community demands high performance and productivity in order to survive. Looking after the health of their employees fosters these goals. The problems associated with poor nutrition and an inactive lifestyle, leading to weight problems, is ubiquitous in the corporate sector. The need to encourage business people to begin and maintain an exercise program has never been more needed and important. The MHP should define his or her expertise with an extensive array of mental health services, but to indicate one *unique* service—fitness coaching—as a particularly valuable and uncommon service.

Educational Institutions

The obesity epidemic has not been relegated to adults; children, adolescents, and college students also suffer from this unfortunate state. Approaching the public school systems, providing in-service training to teachers and coaches, and working in college settings (e.g., at the campus Student Health Center, the Student Recreational Center or Wellness Center) are all needed. Interviews with numerous campus fitness center staff indicate the virtual absence of specialists who provide fitness coaching, particularly in the mental skills and adherence areas. This is sad because so many students do not practice healthy behaviors and are not committed to establishing and maintaining an exercise regimen. They need assistance; this is where the MHP can make a contribution.

Sports

From youth sports leagues to the college level, the area of competitive sport is ripe to receive proper fitness coaching on ways to train properly. Child athletes need information about the proper ways to improve energy and to train properly as one way to gain a performance edge; thus, the motive for exercise is improved sport performance. However, the MHP can improve upon the typical tactics of many coaches by including motivational techniques to make exercise and training enjoyable and meaningful to the performer rather than to burn out the athlete and use exercise as a form of punishment. The athletes' coaches and parents are also in need of fitness coaching, so perhaps the MHP can incorporate a fitness intervention for all family members.

Sports Medicine and Rehabilitation Clinics

As a former consultant in this setting, I can attest to the need for helping patients in overcoming doubt and anxiety about engaging in physical therapy and exercise rehabilitation. Mental health services are also needed in postcardiac and pulmonary rehabilitation programs, in which patients fear that excessive effort will hurt rather than enhance their health. The MHP can provide social support, encouragement, and help patients resolve the inner conflicts of guilt, depression, and anxiety that often accompany chronic illness. Even hospital psychologists that contribute to these programs tend not to have expertise in exercise consulting.

Private Fitness Clubs and Fitness Programs

Fitness clubs are a private business in particular need of MHP consulting. As with any business, profit is a primary motive for survival, while looking after the health of their clients is of secondary importance. This statement is based on my experiences as a former employee in this industry. Thus, ensuring that new members receive proper training and instruction is not an assumption, but rather, requires specialized service. One idea is to establish a private practice within the fitness facility in which all new members receive one complimentary consulting session that is a review of MHP services rendered (e.g., motivation, adherence, self-monitoring checklist review, overcoming exercise barriers, building mental skills). I advise that new members walk away from this initial session with something tangible so that they do not feel the purpose of meeting the MHP was only a sales pitch. I also advise that this person's title not include the words "psychology," "counseling," or "mental." Alternative titles include "performance coach," "fitness advisor," performance/fitness consultant, "coach," or "specialist."

Community Recreation Centers

Public and private recreation centers rarely include exercise coaching. Offering free seminars to the various groups that meet regularly on the Center premises is one way to establish a high profile about private practice. Perhaps Center staff are interested in having MHP service available at selected hours during the week for varying fees to members and nonmembers.

Religious Institutions

Giving free lectures to church, mosque, or synagogue groups has the similar effect of marketing a private practice in fitness coaching. There is ample evidence in scripture that devotion to a higher being is consistent with maintaining proper health. In addition, health is among our most important values, beginning with maintaining a healthy lifestyle.

BUILDING CONSULTATION EXPERTISE

How can the MHP obtain more information in the area of applied exercise psychology? In this section, I review sources of additional knowledge and expertise in this area.

Attending Professional Conferences

A common method of becoming more informed in an area of study and practice is the professional conference in which experts in the field deliver updated research and current thinking. What is unique about the field of applied exercise psychology is that practitioners *should* know something about exercise physiology in order to understand and explain to clients the aspects of training. Incorrect approaches to exercise, for instance, will result in premature fatigue, high perceived exertion, and a resultant unpleasant experience.

While there is no specific conference devoted to applied exercise psychology, there are numerous annual conferences both nationally and internationally that feature the field's top researchers and practitioners. Many of these conferences include and even prioritize sport psychology, in which exercise psychology is an integral part. Examples of organizations with these conferences include the Association for the Advancement of Applied Sport Psychology (AAASP), the American College of Sports Medicine (ACSM), the American Psychological Association (APA; Division 47), American Association of Health, Physical Education, Recreation and Dance (AAHP-ERD), and to a lesser extent, Society of Behavioral Medicine (SBM). Each of these organizations have websites that reveal the dates and venues of annual conferences.

Professional Organizational Memberships

Memberships with related professional organizations result in obtaining materials, reduced fees at annual conferences, and a chance to meet colleagues who conduct research or practice in applied exercise psychology. Examples of organizations that incorporate applied exercise psychology in their respective programs are listed in the preceding section.

Academic Courses

The MHP who lives within driving distance of a university or who can attend pre-conference in-service training sessions and seminars should learn more about this exciting field by registering for courses offered by universities and professional organizations. Many universities offer courses, both undergraduate and graduate, in the area of exercise psychology. An undergraduate exercise physiology course would be another option, since the MHPs needs to understand principles of training and to communicate this to their clients.

Book and Journals

There is a vast array of self-help books on the topic of physical fitness that MHPs should read. Many of these publications are based on sound principles and research. While there are numerous books, some relatively recent, in exercise psychology, none of these can be described as *applied*. However, it remains important for MPHs, whose credibility and expertise is trusted by their clients, to become familiar with this literature and demonstrate mastery in providing guidance. A list of current books and journals is listed in Appendix F, as well as in the reference list of this book.

THE NEED TO OVERCOME OUR OBESITY EPIDEMIC: THE ROLE OF MHPs

There is an enormous and dangerous obesity epidemic in the U.S. and it is taking hold in other countries, as well. Rather than cast blame, the purpose of this section is to articulate the need of MHPs to help combat this growing public health problem through their professional contact with thousands of clients annually. MHPs can have the following roles in improving their client's mental and physical health.

Providing Feedback

The MHP is in the unique position of informing clients that their poor mental (and, perhaps, physical) health may be partially explained by a sedentary lifestyle and the lack of weight control. Very few individuals have the credibility and license to provide this very candid and honest information.

Building Confidence and Optimism

The MHP can help clients build confidence, optimism, and other desirable thought processes that will encourage them to take back control of their lives and their health by improving their lifestyle. Eating for emotional reasons rather than true hunger is a common problem among overweight individuals. Developing new eating and exercise habits will go a long way toward improving quality of life and, of course, contribute markedly to weight loss.

Social Support

The MHP may act as a source of emotional support for their client by offering encouragement, building confidence, sorting out barriers to developing an exercise habit, providing educational materials and other information, make supporting phone calls or e-mails, introduce or refer the client to fitness club personnel, and even meet the client at the exercise venue. Social support can take many forms and is a needed and effective client service.

Revisiting the Values Disconnect Model

Many clients are living a life that is incongruent with their deepest values—their passion and what they consider meaningful in life. The Disconnect Values Model (DVM) (chapter 10) can serve as an intervention template in encouraging clients to examine their life and to live in a manner that is consistent with their values. My own experience with the DVM has been extraordinary in helping people to look introspectively at their negative habits (e.g., no exercise, poor nutrition, overeating, anger, impatience, and so on), and to determine the benefits, the costs, and the long-term consequences of these negative habits on health, happiness, and performance effectiveness. The main thrust of the model, however, is to have the client examine one's values through a checklist. The client then discovers the disconnect(s) between their negative habits and their deepest values and beliefs. It is eye-opening for persons who consider their values sacrosanct, and yet are living a life that is not congruent with those values.

The next stage is also powerful because the individual is asked to determine if this disconnect is acceptable. If it is, then no change is likely to occur; at least, the individual is indicating a nonwillingness to change his or her negative habits to be aligned with their values. However, if the individual considers the costs and long-term consequences of the negative habit(s) unacceptable, and the disconnect(s) from his or her values is undesirable, then the commitment to change is far more forthcoming. The MHP's job is to provide the client with a self-regulatory action plan in which new, positive rituals replace the negative habit(s). Over a 4- to 6-week period, the new rituals should become automatic and performed as part of one's lifestyle.

GAINING CREDIBILITY: WHY MHPS SHOULD EXERCISE

This chapter cannot end without stating the case for MHPs to engage in their own exercise programs. The goal to engage in regular exercise would serve several purposes. First, the MHP would be healthier and have more energy. This outcome would allow the MHP to be more credible when discussing the benefits of a regular exercise program. Second, MHPs would appear healthier and fitter, heeding their own exercise advice. Third, exercising MHPs would have greater, first-hand knowledge of proper exercise technique and be able to provide information based on experience in support of the professional literature. They can inform the client, "This is the way I perform this task, and here is the reason." On a related topic, MHPs may also be an exercise novice, and therefore, empathize with clients who also struggle with generating a new and challenging habit. Fourth, MHPs could use guest passes at local fitness centers to gain first-hand knowledge of their costs, services, quality of facilities, skills of personal trainers to whom to refer clients, and locations.

Finally, it is advised that exercising MHPs generate data that show progress and achievement from their fitness program. Pre-exercise tests might include strength, submaximal VO^2 test (on a treadmill or bicycle ergometer), blood pressure, skinfold measures that reflect percent body fat, and other performance measures that can be compared after a particular time interval and reflects improved scores. Exercising MHPs are credible models from whom clients will feel a special connection and source of inspiration.

Appendix A

Exerciser Checklist

The purpose of this checklist is to provide guidelines for conducting a proper exercise program. This checklist serves the functions of instruction and monitoring progress. It lists desirable thoughts, emotions, and actions that *should* be present before, during, and after your exercise sessions. The checklist is intended to help clients form new positive habits that accompany their exercise routines whether they exercise at a fitness facility or at home. Rate each item ranging from **1** (*not at all like me*) to **5** (*very much like me*). Please be honest because you want to see improvement over time. Higher numbers are always more desirable than lower numbers, however, it is possible some items are unrelated to your preferences and will never change. Your goal should be to reach higher scores (4–5) over time. Try to complete this form regularly, preferably once per week in the beginning, or as often as you wish.

1	2	3	4	5
Not At All Like Me		**Somewhat Like Me**		**Very Much Like Me**

I. Lifestyle Habits (Exercise Preparation)

1. I think about exercising with enthusiasm.	1	2	3	4	5
2. I look forward to my next exercise session.	1	2	3	4	5
3. I do not make excuses for avoiding exercise.	1	2	3	4	5

4. I view exercising as a challenge, not a chore.	1	2	3	4	5
5. I feel healthier and happier for exercising.	1	2	3	4	5
6. I am happy to receive feedback from others on my exercise technique.	1	2	3	4	5
7. I am confident in my ability to exercise.	1	2	3	4	5
8. My family/friends/partner support my exercise habit.	1	2	3	4	5
9. I drink plenty of water during the day.	1	2	3	4	5
10. I schedule my exercise sessions; I know the days and times of the day I will exercise.	1	2	3	4	5
11. I know the physical and psychological benefits of regular exercise.	1	2	3	4	5
12. I think about the positive outcomes of regular exercise.	1	2	3	4	5
13. I usually enjoy the company of others when I exercise.	1	2	3	4	5

Score: _____

1	2	3	4	5
Not At All Like Me		Somewhat Like Me		Very Much Like Me

II. Day of Exercise

1. I look forward to exercising with great enthusiasm.	1	2	3	4	5
2. I am mentally committed to my exercise time.	1	2	3	4	5
3. I am aware of the benefits of my exercise program.	1	2	3	4	5
4. I will not have any food, coffee or alcohol within one hour before I exercise.	1	2	3	4	5
5. If I feel sick, I will not exercise today.	1	2	3	4	5
6. I have a planned route to the exercise venue.	1	2	3	4	5
7. I have prepared my exercise gear in advance.	1	2	3	4	5
8. I have organized my day to accommodate my exercise session.	1	2	3	4	5

Score: _____

1	2	3	4	5
Not At All Like Me		**Somewhat Like Me**		**Very Much Like Me**

III. Pre-Exercise Activity (at exercise venue)

1. I arrive at the exercise venue on time and with enthusiasm.   1 2 3 4 5
2. I have an exercise plan before starting.   1 2 3 4 5
3. I remember my exercise goals and plan to meet them.   1 2 3 4 5
4. As I prepare to exercise, I feel energetic.   1 2 3 4 5
5. I plan to have several water breaks both before and during the exercise routine.   1 2 3 4 5
6. I remember the reasons exercise is good for me.   1 2 3 4 5
7. I complete as much of the exercise session as I can.   1 2 3 4 5
8. I use positive self-talk before exercising ("I can do it," "I'm ready," "Stay with it!")   1 2 3 4 5

Score: _____

1	2	3	4	5
Not At All Like Me		**Somewhat Like Me**		**Very Much Like Me**

IV. During the Exercise Session

1. I really enjoy my exercise session and give 100%.   1 2 3 4 5
2. I stretch lightly *after* I complete light aerobic exercise.   1 2 3 4 5
3. Most of my stretching occurs after my workout.   1 2 3 4 5
4. I use positive self-talk while exercising.   1 2 3 4 5
5. I feel good during warm-up and warm-down exercise.   1 2 3 4 5
6. I complete all the types of exercises I plan to perform.   1 2 3 4 5
7. I complete as many repetitions as possible.   1 2 3 4 5
8. I avoid negative thoughts while exercising.   1 2 3 4 5
9. My exercise performance has improved.   1 2 3 4 5

10.	I do not worry about my appearance during exercise.	1	2	3	4	5
11.	I perform to my potential.	1	2	3	4	5
12.	I view each exercise bout as a challenge, not as a threat to fail.	1	2	3	4	5
13.	I focus my attention external features, not on internal sensations (e.g., fatigue, sweating, discomfort) during the workout.	1	2	3	4	5
14.	I try to reach my performance goals.	1	2	3	4	5
15.	If I feel tired, I rest briefly and then keep going.	1	2	3	4	5
16.	I keep sipping water during my routine.	1	2	3	4	5

Score: _____

1	2	3	4	5
Not At All Like Me		Somewhat Like Me		Very Much Like Me

V.   After the Exercise Session

1.	I am generally pleased with my exercise performance.	1	2	3	4	5
2.	I feel that my performance has improved.	1	2	3	4	5
3.	I have physically or mentally recorded my progress.	1	2	3	4	5
4.	I am open to advice and feedback on my performance.	1	2	3	4	5
5.	I feel a sense of accomplishment.	1	2	3	4	5
6.	I reach my target heart rate (if exercising aerobically).	1	2	3	4	5
7.	I replace my bodily fluids with a lot of water.	1	2	3	4	5
8.	My exercise form has improved.	1	2	3	4	5
9.	I plan to maintain my exercise program.	1	2	3	4	5

Score: _____

GRAND TOTAL: _____

Appendix B

Exercise Tests

MEASURING YOUR PROGRESS

People who engage in an ongoing exercise program often want to observe improvement in their performance. If aerobic fitness, weight control, and other positive outcomes of exercise are to be "meaning-ful" for such individuals, goals must be established and evaluated at some later date. How does one know, for example, if the objective to lose body fat is being met? Persons who feel they can reward themselves for exercising with additional food intake (e.g., an extra dessert or snack) may be storing those "extra" calories. A test that measures percent body fat would be beneficial to determine whether or not the energy balance of calories "in" versus calories "out" has resulted in a loss of fat. Is cardiovascular fitness being enhanced by all of that "huffing and puffing"? The Three-Minute Step Test, which examine one's ability to recover from aerobic work, will tell. Are you taking a "quality" exercise class? Assess yourself (or have an instructor do it) and record your results. Other charts are included in this section which help monitor one's physical activities and motivate exercisers to "stay with it."

SKINFOLD MEASUREMENT

To calculate percent body fat using skinfold measurements (Figure 1), follow the procedures below.

Technique for Taking Skinfolds

1. Take all measurements on the rights side pinching in a vertical line.

2. Grasp the skinfold firmly by the thumb and forefinger.

3. Place the contact surfaces of the calipers $1/2$ inch above the fingers. Release the lever arm on the caliper.

4. Read the dial one to two seconds after releasing your grip.

5. Take each measurement two to three times at each site and then record the average of these measurements on the worksheet provided below (Table B.1).

6. Take the sum of the three skinfolds and refer to Tables B.2 and B.3 to determine the percentage of body fat.

Location of Skinfold Sites

Men (Figure 2)

1. Chest—a diagonal fold located halfway between the right shoulder crease and the nipple.

2. Abdomen—one inch to the right of the navel.

3. Thigh—on the front of the thigh midway between the hip and the knee joint.

TABLE B.1   Worksheet for Determining Percent Body Fat

Men		Women	
Chest	____ mm	Tricep	____ mm
Abdomen	____ mm	Suprailium	____ mm
Thigh	____ mm	Thigh	____ mm
Sum	____ mm	Sum	____ mm
% of Body Fat	____ mm	% of Body Fat	____ mm
Rating	____ mm	Rating	____ mm

TABLE B.2   Percent Fat Estimates for **Women**,* Sum of Triceps, Iliac Crest, and Thigh Skinfolds**

Sum of Skinfolds (mm)	Under 22	23 to 27	28 to 32	33 to 37	38 to 42	43 to 47	48 to 52	53 to 57	Over 58
23–25	9.7	9.9	10.2	10.4	10.7	10.9	11.2	11.4	11.7
26–28	11.0	11.2	11.5	11.7	12.0	12.3	12.5	12.7	13.0
29–31	12.3	12.5	12.8	13.0	13.3	13.5	13.8	14.0	14.3
32–34	13.6	13.8	14.0	14.3	14.5	14.8	15.0	15.3	15.5
35–37	14.8	15.0	15.3	15.5	15.8	16.0	16.3	16.5	16.8
38–40	16.0	16.3	16.5	16.7	17.0	17.2	17.5.	17.7	18.0
41–43	17.2	17.4	17.7	17.9	18.2	18.4	18.7	18.9	19.2
44–46	18.3	18.6	18.8	19.1	19.3	19.6	19.8	20.1	20.3
47–49	19.5	19.7	20.0	20.2	20.5	20.7	21.0	21.2	21.5
50–52	20.6	20.8	21.1	21.3	21.6	21.8	22.1	22.3	22.6
53–55	21.7	21.9	22.1	22.4	22.6	22.9	23.1	23.4	23.6
56–58	22.7	23.0	23.2	23.4	23.7	23.9	24.2	24.4	24.7
59–61	23.7	24.0	24.2	24.5	24.7	25.0	25.2	25.5	25.7
62–64	24.7	25.0	25.2	25.5	35.7	26.0	26.7	26.4	26.7
65–67	25.7	25.9	26.2	26.4	26.7	26.9	27.2	27.4	27.7
68–70	26.6	26.9	27.1	27.4	27.6	27.9	28.1	28.4	28.6
71–73	27.5	27.8	28.0	28.3	28.5	28.8	28.0	29.3	29.5
74–76	28.4	28.7	28.9	29.2	29.4	29.7	29.9	30.2	30.4
77–79	29.3	29.5	39.8	30.0	30.3	30.5	30.8	31.0	31.3
80–82	30.1	30.4	30.6	30.9	31.1	31.4	31.6	31.9	32.1
83–85	30.9	31.2	31.4	31.7	31.9	32.2	32.4	32.7	32.9
36–88	31.7	32.0	32.2	32.5	32.7	32.9	33.2	33.4	33.7
89–91	32.5	32.7	33.0	33.2	33.5	33.7	33.9	34.2	34.4
92–94	33.2	33.4	33.7	33.9	34.2	34.4	34.7	34.9	35.2
95–97	33.9	34.1	34.4	34.6	34.9	35.1	35.4	35.6	35.9
98–100	34.6	34.8	35.1	35.3	35.5	35.8	36.0	36.3	36.5
101–103	35.3	35.4	35.7	35.9	36.2	36.4	36.7	36.9	37.2
104–106	35.8	36.1	36.3	36.6	36.8	37.1	37.3	37.5	37.8
107–109	36.4	36.7	36.9	37.1	37.4	37.6 ·	37.9	38.1	38.4
110–112	37.0	37.2	37.5	37.7	38.0	38.2	38.5	38.7	38.9
113–115	37.5	37.8	38.0	38.2	38.5	38.7	39.0	39.2	39.5
116–118	38.0	38.3	38.5	38.8	39.0	39.3	39.5	39.7	40.0
119–121	38.5	38.7	39.0	39.2	39.5	39.7	40.0	40.2	40.5
122–124	39.0	39.2	39.4	39.7	39.9	40.2	40.4	40.7	40.9
125–127	39.4	39.6	39.9	40.1	40.4	40.6	40.9	41.1	41.4
128–130	39.8	40.0	40.3	40.5	40.8	41.0	41.3	41.5	41.8

*Percent fat calculated by the formula by Siri. Percent fat = $[(4.95/BD - 4.5] \times 100$, where BD = body density.
**Taken from M.L. Pollock, D.H. Schmidt, and A.S. Jackson. "Measurement of Cardiorespiration Fitness and Body Composition in the Clinical Setting." *Comprehensive Therapy, 6* (September 1980): 12–27.

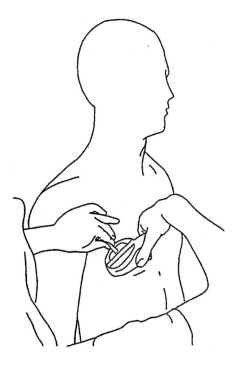

FIGURE 1

Refer to Table B.3 (p. 196) for percent fat estimates.

Women

1. Tricep—on the back of the arm one-half the distance between tip of the shoulder and the tip of the elbow with the arm hanging freely at the side. Figure 3.

2. Thigh—on the front of the thigh, midway between the hip and the knee joint. Figure 4.

3. Suprailium—a slightly oblique fold taken at the top of the iliac crest. Figure 5. Refer to Table B.2 (page 193) for percent fat estimates.

DESIRABLE BODY FAT

Some body fat is considered essential, however, health risks are greater for those with percents body fat in excess of 25% for males and 32% for females.

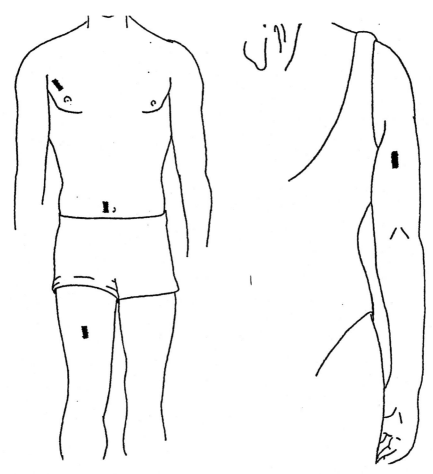

FIGURE 2   FIGURE 3

CALCULATING YOUR TARGET HEART RATE (THR)

(to Obtain or Measure Cardiovascular Fitness)

STEP 1:
Find your maximum heart rate (HR)

Example:

	220		220
–	____	your age	– 20 year-old
=	____	estimated HR max	200

TABLE B.3   Percent Fat Estimates for **Men**,* Sum of Chest, Abdominal, and Thigh Skinfolds**

Sum of Skinfolds (mm)	Under 22	23 to 27	28 to 32	33 to 37	38 to 42	43 to 47	48 to 52	53 to 57	Over 58
8–10	1.3	1.8	2.3	2.9	3.4	3.9	4.5	5.0	5.5
11–13	2.2	2.8	3.3	3.9	4.4	4.9	5.5	6.0	6.5
14–16	3.2	3.8	4.3	4.8	5.4	5.9	6.4	7.0	7.5
17–19	4.2	4.7	5.3	5.8	6.3	6.9	7.4	8.0	8.5
20–22	5.1	5.7	6.2	6.8	7.3	7.9	8.4	8.9	9.5
23–25	6.1	6.6	7.2	7.7	8.3	8.8	9.4	9.9	10.5
26–28	7.0	7.6	8.1	8.7	9.2	9.8	10.3	10.9	11.4
29–31	8.0	8.5	9.1	9.6	10.2	10.7	11.3	11.8	12.4
32–34	8.9	9.4	10.0	10.5	11.1	11.6	12.2	12.8	13.3
35–37	9.8	10.4	10.9	11.5	12.0	12.6	13.1	13.7	14.3
38–40	10.7	11.3	11.8	12.4	12.9	13.5	14.1	14.6	15.2
41–43	11.6	12.2	12.7	13.3	13.8	14.4	15.0	15.5	16.1
44–46	12.5	13.1	13.6	14.2	14.7	15.3	15.9	16.4	17.0
47–49	13.4	13.9	14.5	15.1	15.6	16.2	16.8	17.3	17.9
50–52	14.3	14.8	15.4	15.9	16.5	17.1	17.6	18.2	18.8
53–55	15.1	15.7	16.2	16.8	17.4	17.9	18.5	18.1	19.7
56–58	16.0	16.5	17.1	17.7	18.2	18.8	19.4	20.0	20.5
59–61	16.9	17.4	17.9	18.5	19.1	19.7	20.2	20.8	21.4
62–64	17.6	18.2	18.8	19.4	19.9	20.5	21.1	21.7	22.2
65–67	18.5	19.0	19.6	20.2	20.8	21.3	21.9	22.5	23.1
68–70	19.3	19.9	20.4	21.0	21.6	22.2	22.7	23.3	23.9
71–73	20.1	20.7	21.2	21.8	22.4	23.0	23.6	24.1	24.7
74–76	20.9	21.5	22.0	22.6	23.2	23.8	24.4	25.0	25.5
77–79	21.7	22.2	22.8	23.4	24.0	24.6	25.2	25.8	26.3
80–82	22.4	23.0	23.6	24.2	24.8	25.4	25.9	26.5	27.1
83–85	23.2	23.8	24.4	25.0	25.5	26.1	26.7	27.3	27.9
86–88	24.0	24.5	25.1	25.7	26.3	26.9	27.5	28.1	28.7
89–91	24.7	25.3	25.9	25.5	27.1	27.6	28.2	28.8	29.4
92–94	25.4	26.0	26.6	27.2	27.8	28.4	29.0	29.6	30.2
92–97	26.1	16.7	27.3	27.9	28.5	29.1	29.7	30.3	30.9
98–100	26.9	27.4	28.0	28.6	29.2	29.8	30.4	31.0	31.6
101–103	27.5	28.1	28.7	29.3	29.9	30.5	31.1	31.7	32.3
104–106	28.2	28.8	29.4	30.0	30.6	31.2	31.8	32.4	33.0
107–109	28.9	29.5	30.1	30.7	31.3	31.9	32.5	33.1	33.7
110–112	29.6	30.2	30.8	31.4	32.0	32.6	33.2	33.8	34.4
113–115	30.2	30.8	31.4	32.0	32.6	33.2	33.8	34.5	35.1
116–118	30.9	31.5	32.1	32.7	33.3	33.9	34.5	35.1	35.7
119–121	31.5	32.1	32.7	33.3	33.9	34.5	35.1	35.7	36.4
122–124	32.1	32.7	33.3	33.9	34.5	35.1	35.8	36.4	37.0
125–127	32.7	33.3	33.9	34.5	35.1	35.8	36.4	37.0	37.6

*Percent fat calculated by the formula by Siri.[39] Percent fat = $[(4.95/BD - 4.5] \times 100$, where BD = body density.
**Taken from M.L. Pollock, D.H. Schmidt, and A.S. Jackson, "Measurement of Cardiorespiration Fitness and Body Composition in the Clinical Setting." *Comprehensive Therapy, 6* (September 1980): 12–27. Courtesy of the Laux Co., Inc., Maynard, Mass.

TABLE B.4   Body Fat Norms Based on Percentage of Fat

Classification	Women	Men
Essential Fat	11–14	3–5
Athletes	12–22	5–13
Recreational	16–25	12–18
Potential Risk	26–31	19–24
Obese	32 & above	25 & above

STEP 2:

Find the lower end of your target heart rate zone in beats per minute (bpm).

Example:

```
_____ estimated HR max              200
×  .70                               × .70
_____                             _____
=   _____ bpm                    140.0 bpm
                                     (THR)
                                   (minimum)
```

STEP 3:

Find the upper end of your target heart rate zone in beats per minute.

Example:

```
_____ estimated HR max              200
×  .85                               × .85
_____                             _____
                                      1000
=   _____ bpm                       1600
                                    _____
                                   170.0 bpm
                                 (THR: optimal)
```

My target heart rate range is _____ to _____ beats/minute.

STEP 4:

Find the lower end of your THR in a 10 second count.

_____ ÷ 6 = _____ beats/10 second count.
step 2 answer

Example: 140 ÷ 6 = 23.3

STEP 5:

Find the upper end of your THR in a 10 second count.

_____ ÷ 6 = _____ beats/10 second count.
step 3 answer

Example: 170 ÷ 6 = 28.3

My target heart rate zone is _____ to _____ beats/10 second count.

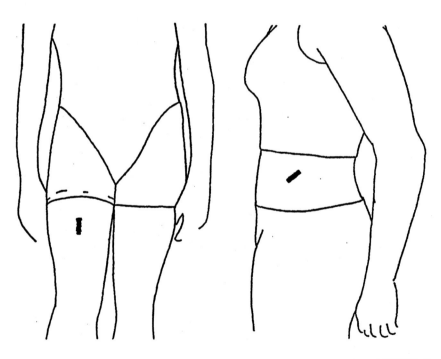

FIGURE 4   FIGURE 5

CARDIORESPIRATORY FITNESS ASSESSMENT

YMCA Three-Minute Step Test

An Estimation of Maximal Oxygen Consumption

Many different versions of the step test are available for use. The step test is based on the premise that for a given submaximal workload, the person with a higher level of cardiovascular fitness will have a *smaller* increase in heart rate, and that following the task the heart rate will return to normal much faster than a person's who has lower cardiovascular fitness.

EQUIPMENT

1. 12-inch-high sturdy bench.

2. Metronome set at 96 beats per minute (4 clicks of the metronome = one step-cycle).

3. Clock to time 3 minutes and the 1-minute recovery.

METHOD

The stepping technique is four counts; one foot up onto the bench (first beat) step up on the second foot (second beat), step down with first foot (third beat), and step down with the other foot (fourth beat).

1. Do not allow the participant to practice, as it will affect the heart rate.

2. The participant steps up and down on bench for 3 minutes keeping with the metronome.

3. Immediately after the 3-minute stepping exercise, the person should sit down.

4. Within 5 seconds the tester should count the radial pulse (at wrist) for 1 FULL MINUTE. The 1-minute count reflects

the heart rate at the end of the exercise plus its ability to quickly recover.

MUSCULAR ENDURANCE

Muscular strength is somewhat dependent on the person's muscular endurance. For example, it takes a certain amount of strength to pick up a suitcase, but it takes a certain amount of muscular endurance to hold that suitcase off the floor for 4 or 5 minutes. If you mention or complain about your "aching muscles" after raking leaves or shoveling snow, you may want to focus on improving your muscular endurance.

Sit-ups are commonly used to assess endurance of the abdominal area, while push-ups usually assess muscular endurance of the upper body, specifically the shoulders, chest, and arms.

BENT KNEE SIT-UPS

Equipment

1. Mat

2. Clock

Method

1. Have the participant lie flat on his or her back with knees bent at 90 degrees and feet flat on the mat approximately 18 inches from buttocks. Cross arms across the chest, resting arms on shoulders.

2. Participant's partner should hold legs still by grasping them at the ankles.

3. Count the number of sit-ups able to be completed in one minute.

4. Refer to Table B.5 (p. 201) for fitness level.

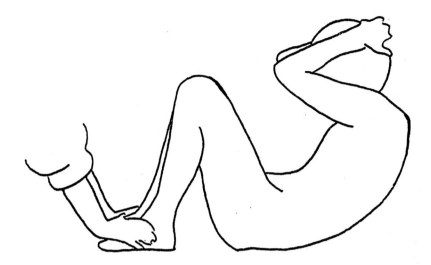

FIGURE 6

TABLE B.5   Fitness Level—Sit-Ups

	Age	Poor	Fair	Average	Good	Excellent
				FITNESS LEVEL—SIT-UPS		
	17-29	0-17	17-35	36-41	42-49	50-55
	30-39	0-13	13-26	27-32	33-39	40-48
Males	40-49	0-11	11-22	23-27	28-35	36-43
	50-59	0-8	7-13	14-19	20-29	30-35
	60-69	0-6	7-13	14-19	20-29	30-35
	17-29	0-14	15-28	29-34	35-42	43-47
	30-39	0-11	12-22	23-29	30-36	37-45
Females	40-49	0-9	10-18	19-25	26-33	34-40
	50-59	0-6	7-12	13-19	20-29	30-35
	60-69	0-5	6-11	12-15	16-24	26-30

PUSH-UPS

Equipment

1. Mat

METHOD

1. **Men:** Start in push-up position with arms straight, fingers forward, trunk and back straight, weight supported on hands and toes.
    Women: Start in push-up position with arms straight, fingers forward, trunk and back straight, weight supported on hands and knees.

2. Have a partner place his or her fist on the floor directly beneath participant's chest.

3. Participant would then lower his/her body until chest touches partner's fist.

4. Count the number of consecutive correctly done push-ups.

5. Refer to Table B.6 for fitness level.

TABLE B.6   Fitness Level—Push-Ups

			FITNESS LEVEL—PUSH-UPS			
	Age	Poor	Fair	Average	Good	Excellent
	15-29	15-19	20-26	27-35	36-45	46-54
Males	30-39	8-14	15-21	22-26	27-34	35-44
	40-49	5-11	12-15	16-20	21-32	33-39
	50-59	3-7	8-13	14-21	22-29	30-34
	60-69	0-4	5-7	8-11	12-21	22-26
	15-29	0-5	6-10	11-20	21-38	39-48
	30-39	0-3	4-9	10-19	20-31	32-38
Females	40-49	0-2	3-6	7-12	13-23	24-32
	50-59	0-1	2-5	6-11	12-20	21-36
	60-69	0	1-2	3-7	8-14	15-20

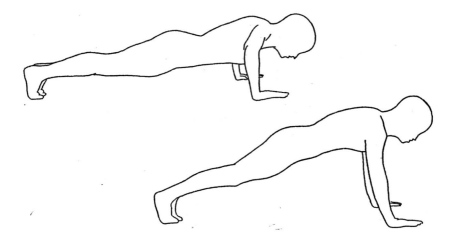

FIGURE 7

FLEXIBILITY

Flexibility encompasses the ability to move a joint through its normal range of motion. To walk a flight of stairs requires some flexibility of the hips, knees, and ankles. It also requires some muscular strength and endurance. Flexibility is also related to strength. Muscles contain strength receptors that help control muscle contractions. When muscles are too tight, the stretch receptors fire too early and cause the muscles to be weaker than they normally would be.

Good trunk flexibility may help protect against low back pain and injury which can be related in part to the tightness of the hamstring muscles, hips, and lower back.

TRUNK FLEXIBILITY

This test measures the flexibility of the lower back muscles and the hip extenders (hamstrings and gluteals).

EQUIPMENT

1. A sit and reach box

METHOD

1. Have participant warm-up properly prior to this test.

2. Participant should refrain from fast, jerky movements that may increase the possibility of an injury.

3. Have participant sit with legs together, knees flat on the floor, and feet flat against sit and reach box.

4. The participant should slowly reach forward with both hands as far as possible over the box and hold this position momentarily.

5. The partner should record the measurement in inches.

6. Record the best of three trials on your Fitness Profile Worksheet and refer to Table B.7 for your fitness rating.

TABLE B.7   Fitness Level—Trunk Flexibility

FITNESS LEVEL—TRUNK FLEXIBILITY						
	Age	Poor	Fair	Average	Good	Excellent
	20-29	0-11	12-14	15-18	19	20+
	30-39	0-10	11-13	14-15	16-17	18+
Males	40-49	0-9	10-12	13-14	15-16	17+
	50-59	0-8	9-11	12-13	14-15	16+
	60+	0-7	8-10	11-12	13-14	15+
	20-29	0-14	15-17	18-20	21	22+
	30-39	0-13	14-16	17-18	19-20	21+
Females	40-49	0-12	13-15	116-17	18-19	20+
	50-59	0-11	12-13	14-15	16-18	19+
	60+	0-10	11-12	13-14	15-17	18+

AEROBIC PROGRESS RECORD

WEEK	TYPE OF ACTIVITY	DURATION OR DISTANCE							WEEKLY TOTALS
		DAY 1	DAY 2	DAY 3	DAY 4	DAY 5	DAY 6	DAY 7	
1									
2									
3									
4									
TOTALS									

INTENSITY _____% to _____%

Target Heart Rate _____% to _____% _____ bpm

10 Second Count _____ to _____

15 Second Count _____ to _____

Examples of Correct Stretches

Complete a 3–5 minute cardiovascular warm-up before stretching.

- Hold each stretch for 15–30 seconds at a point of mild tension.

- Do not bounce, hold in a static manner.

- Maintain regular breathing while stretching.

- With each stretch, make sure to maintain tight abdominals and a pelvic tilt.

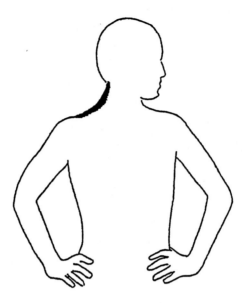

FIGURE 1 **Neck Rotation Stretch:** With back straight and shoulders relaxed slowly turn head toward shoulder. Hold this stretch for 10 seconds, then rotate head toward the opposite shoulder and hold.

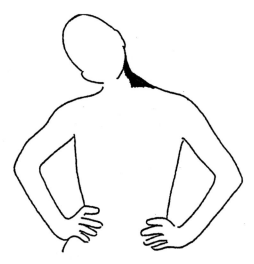

FIGURE 2   **Ear to Shoulder Neck Tilt:** With shoulders relaxed, a pelvic tilt and knees bent, tilt head toward shoulder and hold for 10 seconds. Slowly lift head and repeat on other side.

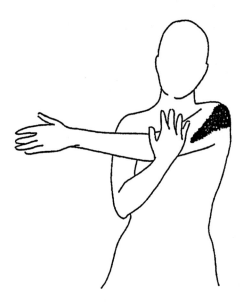

FIGURE 3 **Deltoid Stretch:** Stretch the posterior shoulder muscles. Place one arm across the body at chest height. Place opposite hand above elbow and gently press the extended arm toward the body.

FIGURE 4 **Tricep Stretch:** Extend one arm overhead and drop hand behind head. Take opposite hand and from the front gently press against the back of the arm above elbow.

FIGURE 5 **Shoulder Extensor Stretch:** Stretch the shoulder girdle muscles. Stand with knees bent and a pelvic tilt. Extend arms overhead with palms up and back straight. Gently pull arms back.

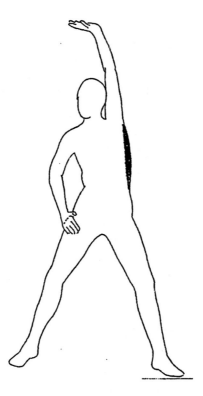

FIGURE 6 **Lateral Stretch:** Stretch the oblique and latissimus dorsi muscles. Stand with knees bent and a pelvic tilt. Extend one arm over head and extend it up and to the side with palm up. Place other hand on hip for support.

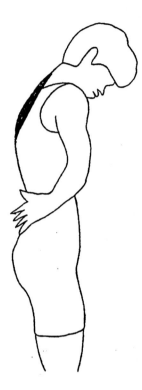

FIGURE 7 **Upper Back Stretch:** Stand with pelvic tilt and knees bent. Place hands on lower back. Keeping hands in place, pull elbows and shoulders to the front, opening the shoulder blades. Bring chin to chest and hold.

FIGURE 8 **Low Back Stretch:** Stretch the erector spinae muscles. Place hands on thighs. Lower your chin to the chest and round the low back by using the abdominal muscles to produce an extreme posterior pelvic tilt.

FIGURE 9 **Chest Stretch:** Stand or sit with abdominals tight and pelvic tilt. Place hands on lower back. Press elbows and shoulders backward. Hold.

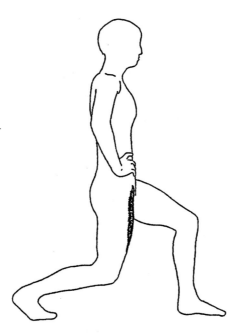

FIGURE 10 **Hip Flexor and Quadricep Stretch:** Keep the rear foot straight and heel on the ground. Shift the body weight forward over the front foot and bend the back leg lifting back heel. Keep the back straight, the buttocks tucked and the pelvis tilted backward.

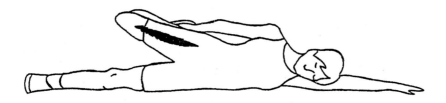

FIGURE 11 **Quadriceps and Hip Flexor Stretch:** Lie on side, with top knee bent. Gently pull foot toward buttocks. Resist with hand on ankle. Keep angle at knees slightly open (do *not* bend knee completely). Hold, then repeat on the other side.

FIGURE 12   **Hamstring Stretch:** Extend one leg in front and lean forward at the waist, using the hands for support on front thigh. Flex front foot.

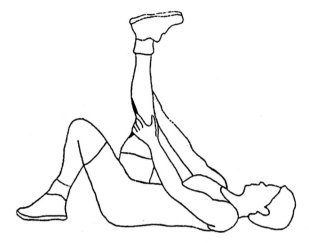

FIGURE 13 **Hamstring Stretch:** Lie on back, knees bent, feet flat on floor. Extend one leg with knee slightly bent, and slowly raise it while keeping abdominals tight. Hold, then repeat on other side.

FIGURE 14 **Inner Thigh Stretch:** To stretch the adductor (inner thigh) muscles, place feet wide apart with toes forward. Shift your weight to one side while bending the knee of weight bearing leg. Hands should be placed on thigh for support. Keep bent knee over toes and lean forward with back straight. Hold position for 10 seconds. Repeat stretch on other side.

FIGURE 15 **Seated Inner Thigh Stretch:** Sit on floor with soles of shoes to-gether, knees out to side. Place hands on floor behind back. Keeping the back straight, press knees towards floor. Hold position for 10–30 seconds.

FIGURE 16 **Outer Thigh Stretch:** Lie on back with feet flat on floor, knees bent. Place left ankle over right knee. Place both hands behind right knee and gently pull toward chest. Hold, then repeat on the other side.

FIGURE 17 **Lower Back Stretch:** Lie on your back and relax your back muscles. Slowly pull one leg in at a time toward the chest. Clasp your hands behind your knees, breathe deeply while relaxing and lengthening the muscles in your lower back. Hold, then repeat.

FIGURE 18 **Gastrocnemius Stretch:** Stretch the calf muscle. Keep rear foot straight and heel on the ground. Shift the body weight forward over the front foot with hands supported on front thigh.

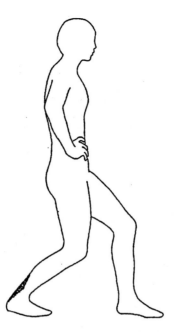

FIGURE 19   **Soleus Stretch:** Keep the rear foot straight and heel on the ground. Center weight over both feet and bend back knee.

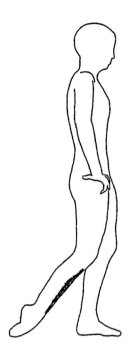

FIGURE 20 **Tibialis Anterior Stretch:** Keep the rear foot straight and place the toe on the ground. Shift the body weight forward over the front foot while you simulate dragging the back toe.

Recommended Books, Journals, and Website Resources

BOOKS

Biddle, S. J. H., Fox, K. R., & Boutcher, S. H. (Eds.). (2000). *Physical activity and psychological well-being*. New York: Routledge.

Dishman, R. K. (1994). *Advances in exercise adherence*. Champaign, IL: Human Kinetics.

Kimiecik, J. (2002). *The intrinsic exerciser: Discovering the joy of exercise*. Boston: Houghton-Mifflin.

Leith, L. M. (1994). *Foundations of exercise and mental health*. Morgantown, WV: Fitness Information Technology.

Mackinnon, L. T., Ritchie, C. B., Hooper, S. L., & Abernethy, P. J. (2003). *Exercise management: Concepts and professional practice*. Champaign, IL: Human Kinetics.

Marcus, B. H., & Forsyth, L. H. (2003). *Motivating people to be physically active*. Champaign, IL: Human Kinetics.

Seraganian, P. (Ed.). (1993). *Exercise psychology: The influence of physical exercise on psychological processes*. New York: John Wiley & Sons.

Shumaker, S. A., Schron, E. B., Ockene, J. K., & McBee, W. L. (Eds.). (1998). *The handbook of health behavior change* (2nd ed.). New York: Springer.

JOURNALS

American Journal of Health Promotion
Annals of Behavioral Medicine
Health Psychology
International Journal of Sport Psychology

International Journal of Sport and Exercise Psychology
Journal of Applied Sport Psychology
Journal of Behavioral Medicine
Journal of Health Psychology
Journal of Health and Social Behavior
Journal of Physical Activity and Health
Journal of Psychosomatic Research
Journal of Sport and Exercise Psychology
Journal of Sport Behavior
Journal of Sport Sciences
Medicine and Science in Sport and Exercise
Psychology of Sport and Exercise
Research Quarterly for Exercise and Sport
The Sport Psychologist

WEBSITES

American College of Sports Medicine (ACSM): www.acsm.org

American Psychological Association (APA)
   APA Division 47 (Sport and Exercise Psychology): www.psyc.unt.edu/apadiv47
   APA Division 38 (Health Psychology): www.health-psych.org

Association for the Advancement of Applied Sport Psychology (AAASP): www.aaasponline.org

Canadian Society for Psychomotor Learning and Sport Psychology (SCAPPS): www.scapps.org

Centers for Disease Control (CDC): www.cdc.gov

European Federation of Sport Psychology (FEPSAC): www.psychology.lu.se/fepsac

International Society of Sport Psychology (ISSP): www.issponlone.org

National Sleep Foundation (NSF): www.nationalsleepfoundation.org

Society of Behavioral Medicine (SBM): www.sbmweb.org

List of Organizations and Publications

Here is a list of the professional organizations that include exercise psychology content at their conferences and publications. Also included are resources to keep fitness professionals updated on current trends and literature in the field, as well as specific certifications.

Aerobics and Fitness Association of America (AFAA)
1520 Ventura Boulevard, Suite 200
Sherman Oaks, CA 91403
(800) 446-2322 or (919) 905-0040

American Aerobic Association/International Sports Medicine Association (AAA/ISMA)
P.O. Box 633
Richboro, PA 18954

American College of Sports Medicine (ACSM)
P.O. Box 1440
Indianapolis, IN 46206
(317) 637-9200
www.acsm.org

American Council on Exercise (ACE)
P.O. Box 910449
San Diego, CA 92191-0449
(800) 825-3636 or (619) 535-8227

American Psychological Association (APA)
Division 38 (Health Psychology)
www.health-psych.org

American Psychological Association (APA)
Division 47 (Sport and Exercise Psychology)
www.psyc.unt.edu/apadiv47

Aquatic Exercise Association
P.O. Box 497
Port Washington, WI 53074
(414) 284-3416

Association for the Advancement of Applied Sport Psychology (AAASP)
Website: www.aaasponline.org

AVIA's Select Direct Instructor
Discount Purchase Program
(800) 275-3565

Canadian Society for Psychomotor Learning and Sport Psychology (SCAPPS)
www.scapps.org

Cooper Institute for Aerobic Research
12330 Preston Rd.
Dallas, TX 75230
(800) 635-7050

Exer-Safety Association
10151 University Blvd. Suite 138
Orlando, FL 32817
(407) 677-9501

European Foundation of Sport Psychology (FEPSAC)
www.psychology.lu.se/fepsac

Fitness Awareness C.E.C. Training Inc. (FACT)
134 Willow Avenue
Deerfield, IL 60015
(800) 876-FACT or (708) 498-FACT

IDEA: The Association for Fitness Professional
6190 Cornerstone Court East, Suite 204
San Diego, CA 92121-3773
(619) 535-8979

International Society of Sport Psychology (ISSP)
www.ISSPonline.org

NIKE Instructor Discount Program
One Bowerman Drive
Beaverton, OR 97005
(800) 344-6453

Reebok Professional Instructor Alliance
100 Technology Drive
Stoughton, MA 02072
(800) 435-7022

RYKA Training Body Instructor Discount Program
249 Oceana Way
Norwood, MA 02062
(800) 255-RYKA

Sara's City Workout, Inc./Mania Events
P.O. Box 268165
Chicago, IL 60626
(800) 545-CITY

References

Ades, P. A., Waldmann, M. L., McCann, W. J., & Weaver, S. O. (1992). Predictors of cardiac rehabilitation in older coronary patients. *Archives of Internal Medicine, 152*, 1033–1035.

Ajzen, I. (1985). From intention to actions: A theory of planned behavior. In J. Kuhl & J. Beckman (Eds.), *Action control: From cognition to behavior* (pp. 11–39). Heidelberg, Germany: Springer.

Ajzen, I., & Fishbein, M. (1974). Factors influencing intentions and the intention-behavior relation. *Human Relations, 27*, 1–15.

American College of Sports Medicine (ACSM). (2001). *ACSM's resource manual for guidelines for exercise testing and prescription* (4th ed.). Philadelphia: Lippincott, Williams, & Williams.

American Psychiatric Association. (1994). *Diagnostic and statistical manual of mental disorders: DSM-IV, 4th ed.* Washington, DC: American Psychiatric Association.

Anshel, M. H. (2003a, August 7–10). *Effect of a values-based model on promoting exercise adherence.* Presented at the Annual Convention of the American Psychological Association, Toronto (Canada).

Anshel, M. H. (2003b). *Sport psychology: From theory to practice* (4th ed.). San Francisco: Benjamin-Cummings.

Anshel, M. H. (Ed.), Freedson, P., Hamill, J., Haywood, K., Horvat, M., & Plowman, S. A. (1991). *Dictionary of the sport and exercise sciences.* Campaign, IL: Human Kinetics.

Anshel, M. H., & Marisi, D. Q. (1978). Effect of music and rhythm on physical performance. *Research Quarterly, 49*, 109–113.

Anshel, M. H., & Reeves, L. H. (1998). *Aerobics for fitness* (5th ed.). Boston, MA: Pearson Education.

Anshel, M. H., Reeves, L. H., & Roth, R. R. (2003). *Concepts in fitness: A balanced approach to good health.* Boston: Pearson Education.

Anshel, M. H., & Russell, K. (1994). Effect of aerobic and strength training on pain tolerance, pain appraisal and mood of unfit males as a function of pain location. *Journal of Sports Sciences, 12*, 535–547.

Anshel, M. H., Seipel, S., & Anderson, P. (March 24–27, 2004). *Self-monitoring promotes exercise adherence over an eight-week summer program among university faculty.* Presented at the Conference of the Society for Behavioral Medicine, Baltimore, MD.

Bandura, A. (1997). *Self-efficacy: The exercise of control.* New York: Freemen.

Baranowski, T., Anderson, C., & Carmack, C. (1998). Mediating variable framework in physical activity interventions. How are we doing? How might we do better? *American Journal of Preventive Medicine, 15*, 266–297.

Becker, M. H., & Maiman, L. A. (1975). Sociobehavioral determinants of compliance with health and medical care recommendations. *Medical Care, 13*, 10–24.

Berger, B. G., Pargman, D., & Weinberg, R. S. (2002). *Foundations of exercise psychology.* Morgantown, WV: Fitness Information Technology.

Berger, B. G., & Motl, R. W. (2000). Exercise and mood: A selective review and synthesis of research employing the profile of mood states. *Journal of Applied Sport Psychology, 12*, 69–92.

Berle, M. (March 31, 2002). *Orlando Sentinel,* p. C2.

Biddle, S. J. H., & Mutrie, N. (2001). *Psychology of physical activity: Determinants, well-being, and interventions.* New York: Routledge.

Blair, S. N., & Brodney, S. (1999). Effects of physical inactivity and obesity on morbidity and mortality: Current evidence and research issues. *Medicine and Science in Sports and Exercise, 31*, S646–S662.

Borg, G. A. (1998). *Borg's perceived exertion and pain scales.* Champaign, IL: Human Kinetics.

Brawley, L. R. (1993). The practicality of fusing social psychological theories for exercise and health research and intervention. *Journal of Applied Sport Psychology, 5*, 99–115.

Brown, D., & Crace, R. K. (1996). Values in life role choices and outcomes: A conceptual model. *Career Development Quarterly, 44*, 21–223.

Buckworth, J., & Dishman, R. K. (2002). *Exercise psychology.* Champaign, IL: Human Kinetics.

Bull, S. J., Albinson, J. G., & Shambrook, C. J. (1996). *The mental game plan: Getting psyched for sport.* Eastbourne, UK: Sports Dynamics.

Clark, N. M., & Becker, M. H. (1998). Theoretical models and strategies for improving adherence and disease management. In S. A. Shumaker, E. B. Schron, J. K. Ockene, & W. L. McBee (Eds.), *The handbook of health behavior change* (2nd ed., pp. 5–32). New York: Springer.

Cockerill, I. M., & Riddington, M. E. (1996). Exercise dependence and associated disorders: A review. *Counseling Psychology Quarterly, 9*, 119–129.

Corbin, C., & Lindsay, R. (2005). *Fitness for life* (5th ed.). Campaign, IL: Human Kinetics.

Crace, R. K., & Hardy, C. J. (1997). Individual values and the team building process. *Journal of Applied Sport Psychology, 9*, 41–60.

Crews, D. J., & Landers, D. M. (1987). A meta-analysis review of aerobic fitness and reactivity to psychosocial stressors. *Medicine and Science in Sports and Exercise, 19*, S114–S120.

Deci, E. L. (1975). *Intrinsic motivation.* New York: Plenum.

Dunn, A. L., Andersen, R. E., & Jakicic, J. M. (1998). Lifestyle physical activity interventions. History, short- and long-term effects, and recommendations. *American Journal of Preventive Medicine, 15*, 398–412.

Dunn, A. L., Trivedi, M. H., Kampert, J. B., Clark, C. G., & Chambliss, H. O. (2005). Exercise treatment for depression: Efficacy and dose response. *American Journal of Preventive Medicine, 28*, 1–8.

Folkins, C. H., & Sime, W. E. (1981). Physical fitness training and mental health. *American Psychologist, 36*, 373–389.

Gauvin, L., Levesque, L., & Richard, L. (2001). Helping people initiate and maintain a more active lifestyle: A public health framework for physical activity promotion research. In R. N. Singer, H. A. Hausenblas, & C. M. Janelle (Eds.), *Handbook of sport psychology* (2nd ed., pp. 718–739). New York: John Wiley & Sons, Inc.

Glasgow, R. E., Klesges, L. M., Dzewaltowski, D. A., Bull, S. S., & Estabrooks, P. (2004). The future of health behavior change research: What is needed to improve translation of research into health promotion practice. *Annals of Behavioral Medicine, 27,* 3–12.

Glasser, W. (1976). *Positive addiction.* New York: Harper & Row.

Groppel, J. (2000). *The corporate athlete.* New York: John Wiley & Sons.

Haan, N., Aerts, E., & Cooper, B. A. B. (1985). *On moral grounds: The search for practical morality.* New York: New York University Press.

Hausenblas, H. A., Carron, A. V., & Mack, D. E. (1997). Application of the theories of reasoned action and planned behavior to exercise behavior: A meta-analysis. *Journal of Sport and Exercise Psychology, 19,* 36–51.

Hogan, H. W., & Mookherjee, H. N. (1981). Values and selected antecedents. *Journal of Social Psychology, 113,* 29–35.

Hollander, E. P. (1967). *Principles and methods of social psychology.* New York: Holt, Rinehart, & Winston.

Jung, A. P., & Nieman, D. C. (2000). An evaluation of home exercise equipment claims: Too good to be true. *ACSM's Health & Fitness Journal, 4,* 14–16.

Kobassa, S. C. (1979). Stressful life events, personality, and health: An inquiry into hardiness. *Journal of Personality and Social Psychology, 37,* 1–11.

Lavizzo-Mourey, R. J. (March 24–27, 2004). *Childhood obesity.* Presented at the Society of Behavioral Medicine Conference, Baltimore, MD.

Leith, L. M. (1994). *Foundations of exercise and mental health.* Morgantown, WV: Fitness Information Technology.

Leith, L. M. (1998). *Exercise your way to better mental health.* Morgantown, WV: Fitness Information Technology.

Loehr, J., & Schwartz, T. (2003). *The power of full engagement: Managing energy, not time, is the key to high performance and personal renewal.* New York: Free Press.

Lox, C. L., Martin, K. A., & Petruzzello, S. J. (2003). *The psychology of exercise: Integrating theory and practice.* Scottsdale, AZ: Holcomb Hathaway.

Mackinnon, L. T., Ritchie, C. B., Hooper, S. L., & Abernethy, P. J. (2003). *Exercise management: Concepts and professional practice.* Champaign, IL: Human Kinetics.

Marcus, B. H., & Forsythe, L. H. (2003). *Motivating people to be physically active.* Champaign, IL: Human Kinetics.

Markland, D. (1999). Self-determination moderates the effects of perceived competence on intrinsic motivation in an exercise setting. *Journal of Sport and Exercise Psychology, 21,* 351–361.

Markland, D., & Ingledew, D. K. (1997). The measurement of exercise motives: Factorial validity and invariance across gender of a revised Exercise Motivation Inventory. *British Journal of Health Psychology, 2,* 361–376.

Marlatt, G. A., & Gordon, J. R. (1985). *Relapse prevention: Maintenance strategies in addictive behavior change*. New York: Guilford Press.

McAuley, E., & Mihalko, S. L. (1998). Measuring exercise-related self-efficacy. In J. L. Duda (Ed.), *Advances in sport and exercise psychology measurement* (pp. 371–392). Morgantown, WV: Fitness Information Technology.

Miller, N. H., Hill, M., Koftke, T., & Ockene, I. S. (1997). The multilevel compliance challenge: Recommendations for a call to action. A statement for healthcare professionals. *Circulation, 95*, 1085–1090.

Mondin, G. W., Morgan, W. P., Piering, P. N., & Stegner, A. J. (1996). Psychological consequences of exercise deprivation in habitual exercisers. *Medicine and Science in Sports, 28*, 1199–1203.

National Sleep Foundation (2002). Website: www.nationalsleepfoundation.org/publications

Nestle, M., & Jacobson, M. F. (January/February, 2000). Halting the obesity epidemic: A public health policy approach. *Public Health Reports, 115*, 12–24.

Nicassio, P. M., Meyerowitz, B. E., & Kerns, R. D. (2004). The future of health psychology interventions. *Health Psychology, 23*, 132–137.

Nieman, D. C. (2003). *Exercise testing and prescription: A health-related approach* (5th ed.). New York: McGraw-Hill.

North, T. C., McCullagh, P., & Va Tran, Z. (1990). Effect of exercise on depression. *Exercise and Sport Sciences Reviews, 18*, 379–415.

O'Connor, P. J., & Davis, J. C. (1992). Psychobiologic responses to exercise at different times of day. *Medicine and Science in Sports and Exercise, 24*, 714–719.

Okene, J. K. (2001). Strategies to increase adherence to treatment. In L. E. Burke & I. S. Ockene (Eds.), *Compliance in healthcare and research* (pp. 43–56). Armonk, NY: Futura Publishing.

Oldridge, N. B. (2001). Future directions: What paths do researchers need to take? What needs to be done to improve multi-level compliance? In L. E. Burke & I. S. Ockene (Eds.), *Compliance in healthcare and research* (pp. 331–347). Armonk, NY: Futura Publishing.

Oldridge, N. B., & Streiner, D. L. (1990). The health belief model: Predicting compliance and dropout in cardiac rehabilitation. *Medicine and Science in Sports and Exercise, 22*, 678–683.

Paternoster, R. (1987). The deterrent effect of the perceived certainty and severity of punishment: A review of the evidence and issues. *Justice Quarterly, 4*, 173–217.

Pearson, T. A., & Kopin, L. A. (2001). Compliance of providers to guidelines. In L. E. Burke & I. S. Ockene (Eds.), *Compliance in healthcare and research* (pp. 285–298). Armonk, NY: Futura Publishing.

Petruzzello, S. J., Landers, D. M., Hatfield, B. D., Kubitz, K. A., & Salazar, W. (1991). A meta-analysis on the anxiety-reducing effects of acute and chronic exercise: Outcomes and mechanisms. *Sports Medicine, 11*, 143–182.

Prochaska, J. O., & DiClemente, C. C. (1983). Stages and processes of self-change n smoking: Towards an integrative model of change. *Journal of Consulting and Clinical Psychology, 51*, 390–395.

Prochaska, J. O., & Marcus, B. (1994). The transtheoretical model: Applications to exercise. In R. K. Dishman (Ed.), *Advances in exercise adherence* (pp. 161–180). Champaign, IL: Human Kinetics.

Rand, C. S., & Weeks, K. (1998). Measuring adherence with medication regimens in clinical care and research. In S. A. Shumaker, E. B. Schron, J. K. Ockene, & W. L. McBee (Eds.), *The handbook of health behavior change* (2nd ed., pp. 114–132). New York: Springer.

Ray, R., & Weise-Bjornstad, D. M. (1999). *Counseling in sports medicine.* Champaign, IL: Human Kinetics.

Rokeach, M. (1973). *The nature of human values.* New York: Free Press.

Rosen, C. S. (2000). Is the sequencing of change processes by stage consistent across health problems? A meta-analysis. *Health Psychology, 19,* 593–604.

Rowland, T. W. (2005). *Children's exercise physiology* (2nd ed.). Champaign, IL: Human Kinetics.

Sackett, D. L. (1976). The magnitude of compliance and noncompliance. In K. L. Sackett & R. B. Haynes (Eds.), *Compliance with therapeutic regimens* (pp. 9–25). Baltimore: Johns Hopkins University Press.

Sallis, J. F., & Hovell, M. F. (1990). Determinants of exercise behavior. *Exercise and Sport Sciences Reviews, 11,* 307–330.

Sallis, J. F., & Owen, N. (1999). *Physical activity & behavioral medicine.* Thousand Oaks, CA: Sage.

Sarafino, E. P. (1994). *Health psychology: Biopsychosocial interactions* (2nd ed.). New York: John Wiley & Sons.

Schlenk, E. A., Burke, L. E., & Rand, C. (2001). Behavioral strategies to improve medication-taking compliance. In L. E. Burke & I. S. Ockene (Eds.), *Compliance in healthcare and research* (pp. 57–70). Armonk, NY: Futura Publishing Company.

Strelan, P., & Boeckmann, R. J. (2003). A new model for understanding performance-enhancing drug use by elite athletes. *Journal of Applied Sport Psychology, 15,* 176–183.

Super, D. E. (1995). Values: Their nature, assessment, and practical use. In D. E. Super & B. Sverko (Eds.), *Life roles, values, and careers: International findings of the work importance study* (pp. 54–61). San Francisco: Jossey-Bass.

Treasure, D. C., & Newbery, D. M. (1998). Relationship between self-efficacy, exercise intensity and feeling states in a sedentary population during and following an acute bout of exercise. *Journal of Sport and Exercise Psychology, 20,* 1–12.

Wallston, K. A., Smith, R. A., & King, J. E. (1983). Expectancies about control over health: Relationships to desire for control of health care. *Personality & Social Psychology Bulletin, 9,* 377–385.

Wenger, N. K. (1995). Future directions in cardiac rehabilitation. In M. L. Pollock & D. H. Schmidt (Eds.), *Heart disease and rehabilitation* (3rd ed., pp. 447–453). Champaign, IL: Human Kinetics.

White, R. W. (1959). Motivation reconsidered: The concept of competence. *Psychological Review, 66,* 297–331.

Index